Splendid Food

SPLENDID FOOD

Irish Country Houses

GUIDE AND RECIPES

GILLIAN BERWICK

Introduction by
MYRTLE ALLEN

Illustrated by
JEREMY WILLIAMS

THE O'BRIEN PRESS
DUBLIN

This edition first published 1990 by The O'Brien Press Ltd.,
20 Victoria Road, Rathgar, Dublin 6, Ireland.
First published in hardback by Berwick Publishers.

British Library Cataloguing in Publication data:
Berwick, Gillian
Splendid Food: Irish Country Houses, Guide and Recipes.
1. Food: Irish dishes – Recipes
2. Ireland. Country Houses. Visitors' Guides
I. Title
641.59415

ISBN 0-86278-222-8

10 9 8 7 6 5 4 3 2 1

Cookery Consultant: Myrtle Allen.
Cover illustrations: Donald Teskey
Typeset at The O'Brien Press
Separations: The City Office, Dublin
Printing: Guernsey Press Co Ltd

I wish to express my indebtedness to
the many owners of the hotels and restaurants as
well as friends and colleagues who
have given me their time, assistance and
encouragement to produce the material
for this book.

By the same author
Making Your Own Chocolates
A Cook's Tour of Dublin

Contents

Moyglare Manor 12

Hunter's Hotel 17

Tinakilly House 21

The Old Rectory 25

Rathsallagh House 30

Doyle's Schoolhouse Restaurant 35

Marlfield House 40

Step House Restaurant 45

Aherne's Seafood Bar 49

Ballymaloe House 52

Longueville House and Presidents' Restaurant 57

Assolas Country House 61

Blairs Cove 67

Ballylickey Manor House 71

The Park Hotel 75

Doyle's Seafood Bar 80

MacCloskey's 84

Gregans Castle Hotel 88

Drimcong House Restaurant 92

Currarevagh House 96

Cashel House 101

Rosleague Manor 106

Newport House 111

Enniscoe House 117

Mount Falcon Castle 121

Coopershill House 125

Reveries Restaurant 130

Ernan Park 135

Rathmullan House 140

Blackheath House 145

Index 152

Location Map 157

Restaurants by alphabetical order

Aherne's Seafood Bar – 163 North Main Street, Youghal, Co. Cork 49

Assolas Country House – Kanturk, Co. Cork 61

Ballylickey Manor House – Bantry Bay, Co. Cork 71

Ballymaloe House – Shanagarry, Midleton, Co. Cork 52

Blackheath House – 112 Killeague Road, Blackhill, Coleraine, Co. Londonderry 145

Blairs Cove– Durrus, Nr Bantry, Co. Cork 67

Cashel House – Cashel, Co. Galway 101

Coopershill House – Riverstown, Co. Sligo 125

Currarevagh House – Oughterard, Connemara, Co. Galway 96

Doyle's Schoolhouse Restaurant – Castledermot, Co. Kildare 35

Doyle's Seafood Bar – John Street, Dingle, Co. Kerry 80

Drimcong House Restaurant – Moycullen, Co. Galway 92

Enniscoe House, Castlehill – Nr Crossmolina, Ballina, Co. Mayo 117

Ernan Park, St Ernan's Island – Nr Donegal town, Co. Donegal 135

Gregans Castle Hotel – Ballyvaughan, Co. Clare 88

Hunter's Hotel – Rathnew, Co. Wicklow 17

Longueville House & Presidents' Restaurant – Mallow, Co. Cork 57

MacCloskey's – Bunratty House Mews, Co. Clare 84

Marlfield House – Gorey, Co. Wexford 40

Mount Falcon Castle – Ballina, Co. Mayo 121

Moyglare Manor – Maynooth, Co. Kildare 12

Newport House – Newport, Co. Mayo 111

Old Rectory, The – Wicklow, Co. Wicklow 25

Park Hotel, The – Kenmare, Co. Kerry 75

Rathmullan House – Rathmullan, Co. Donegal 140

Rathsallagh House – Dunlavin, Co. Wicklow 30

Reveries Restaurant – Rosses Point, Sligo 130

Rosleague Manor – Letterfrack, Co. Galway 106

Step House Restaurant – Borris, Co. Carlow 45

Tinakilly House – Rathnew, Co. Wicklow 21

Foreword

GILLIAN BERWICK WAS BROUGHT UP in Australia, but she travelled the world several times during her teens on business trips with her family, invariably staying at famous hotels wherever they went.

After college Gillian studied cookery and went into business in this field in Australia. In 1985 she decided to further her cookery studies in Ireland, and was later joined by her parents. They took apartments in one of the great private country houses of the Midlands. The house and the cookery school made a double impression on Gillian, so she had this good idea of presenting, in book form, the food and buildings of the present-day large country houses in Ireland. She chose houses which are open to the public and are grouped together in a single organisation which accepts only those with the highest standards – the Irish Country House and Restaurant Association. Here she found a new dimension in the world of hotels. Jeremy Williams, the architect and artist who is most closely associated with the restoration and maintenance of these houses, travelled the country with her to illustrate this book. Nobody more than Jeremy cares for or can capture the charm that makes each house unique and individual. There is no streaming into a marketable uniformity here, simply individuals in their own homes, free to equip, decorate and run their premises as they choose, and to share it with those who want a real glimpse of Ireland.

The only obligatory standards they must share is a high degree of comfort and service to provide a good table. You will see that this is no cottage cookery book; the occupants of 'the big house' have always served sophisticated food and known how to adapt new recipes from abroad to the good Irish ingredients. In this case each recipe has been left virtually as the owner or chef contributed it. If you are puzzled with one – write to the house directly, or better still, pay a visit and taste it there!

Myrtle Allen,
BALLYMALOE HOUSE, SHANAGARRY, CO. CORK.

Introduction

IRISH COUNTRY HOUSES have always had one thing in common – hospitality is paramount. In Ireland, this tradition goes back to ancient times when the traveller, bard or stranger was watched for and welcomed as one who carried tidings from far and wide. When he arrived he was the centre and focus of attention, to be served with the best while he gave his news. Whether the country house was a castle or a mansion, a priory or a cottage, the reaction was the same. This, in part, explains the special welcome received by visitors to the Irish Country House Hotels and Restaurants.

Throughout the centuries, Ireland has exported people like the Swiss today export 'Swatches'. All over the globe, in America, Australia, Canada, people have 'come from' Ireland. My interest in Irish country houses blossomed when I came to Ireland from Australia – a Swatch in reverse! and began living in one. I became obsessed with history, styles and periods. I automatically looked up at the ceiling when I walked into a strange room, admiring the craftsmanship of some past artisan. I mused about the great Irish literary figures of the past, from Goldsmith, Swift and Moore to Yeats and Shaw and wondered how many had graced these rooms.

Being a cookery writer, however, my enthusiasm finally focused on the kitchens and I wanted to share my experiences of Irish Country House hotels with all who visit or return searching for a taste of Ireland.

From times past the country houses have always had their walled gardens for fruit and vegetables, well stocked greenhouses and a bountiful supply of fresh herbs. Pickles, jams and other preserves were made and stored, but vegetables were, of necessity, always served according to what was 'in season'. As this tradition, thankfully, remains, I have omitted vegetables from most menus.

I am grateful for the enthusiasm with which my proposal to write an Irish country house cookbook was received by the proprietors. I have been given first-hand experience of their Irish hospitality and can vouch for the professionalism of their enterprises and the acclaimed cuisine for which many of them have won prestigious international awards.

These are not my own recipes, but contributions generously given to me to use in my book by the individual chefs of the ICHRA.

Gillian Berwick,
Emo Court, Emo, Co. Laois.

Unless otherwise stated, all recipes serve six people. Prices refer to a 1990 rate for an average meal, and dinner times are for first and last orders.

Moyglare Manor

THIS ELEGANT GEORGIAN HOUSE has been handsomely furnished with a profusion of antiques, paintings and oriental rugs by owner Norah Devlin. The main drawing room, with plasterwork ceiling (attributed to Michael Stapleton) and rich burgundy red walls, is a particularly lovely room. Each bedroom is immaculately kept, comfortably furnished with antiques and carefully chosen fabrics. Here I saw a lady on her hands and knees combing rug frills to make sure they were straight! There is a club-like bar with a blazing fire which is a focal point for guests but there are many other small public rooms for those who prefer solitude. The restaurant is fully licensed and the food highly recommended. Maynooth is an historic university and market town in Co. Kildare, Ireland's world famous horse breeding and training county. The rural bliss of Moyglare is only 18 miles from Dublin.

Moyglare Manor, Moyglare, Maynooth, Co. Kildare.
Tel: 01-286351/286469. Fax: 01-285405.

Reservations: Robert Reid Associates
Proprietor: Mrs Norah Devlin
Open all year except three days at Christmas.
Children under 12 not catered for.
How to find
Travelling west on N4, through Maynooth,
keep right at Church – 2 km.
Restaurant
Table d'hôte dinner IR£18.50.
À la carte dinner (Sat. night only) 7.00-9.30 pm. 12½% service charge.
Lunch 12.30-2.15 from IR£9.95.
No Saturday lunch. Booking only for lunch/dinner.
Accommodation
Four-posters (incl. full Irish breakfast) IR£47.50 per person sharing.
Garden suite (incl. full Irish breakfast) IR£50.00 per person sharing.
IR£15.00 single supplement.
No. of bedrooms: 17 (incl. garden suite).
All major credit cards accepted.
French spoken.

Moyglare Manor, built in 1775, is supposedly the Dower
House to the nearby Carton Estate. It was bought as a family home
and refurbished as an hotel in the last five years
by owner Norah Devlin.

Carrot and Onion Soup

3 lb (1.4 k) carrots
2 lb (900 g) potatoes
1 onion
8 fl oz (250 ml)/1 cup fresh orange juice
4 pints (2.4 l)/10 cups chicken stock
1 pint (600 ml)/2½ cups milk or milk and cream
2 oz (55 g)/¼ cup butter
salt and pepper

Roughly chop all vegetables. Sweat in melted butter for 10 minutes. Add chicken stock and seasoning. Cook until vegetables are soft. Liquidise, add orange juice and return to heat. Blend in milk and cream.

Pigeon Pie

Puff pastry
6 pigeon breasts
10 oz (300 g) of beef
6 oz (170 g) of streaky bacon
¼ pint (150 ml)/⅝ cup of red wine
½ pint (300 ml)/1¼ cups of chicken stock
sprig of thyme and parsley
2 cloves garlic
1 large onion, chopped
¼ pint (150 g) tomato purée
3 tablespoons vegetable oil

Slice beef and pigeon breasts into ½ inch (1¼ cm) strips. Slice the bacon, onion and crush the garlic. Toss all in a heavy casserole with oil for about five minutes. Remove from pan and add wine, stock and tomato purée. Reduce for about 2 minutes. Add all ingredients and season. Cover and place in a moderate oven for one hour. Remove from oven, thicken with an ounce of roux, place in oven dish, cover with puff pastry and return to oven for 15 minutes.

Chocolate Profiteroles with Banana Cream

Choux Pastry

2 oz (55 g)/¼ cup butter
8 fl oz (250 ml)/1 cup water
5 oz (140 g)/1 cup flour
3-4 eggs

Preheat the oven to 350°F/180°C/Regulo 4.
Bring butter and water almost to the boil, add the flour and cook
for 1½ minutes, stirring all the time. Gradually beat in the eggs
until consistency is thick and shiny. Using a ⅜ inch nozzle, put the
mixture in a piping bag and pipe into small profiterole shapes on a
lightly greased baking tray. Cook for 20 minutes, prick pastry and
return to the oven for a further 5-10 minutes until dried out.
Remove and allow to cool.

Filling

5 fl oz (150 ml)/⅔ cup whipped cream
1 banana, liquidised
juice of ½ lemon
brandy to taste

Blend all the ingredients and pipe into the profiteroles. Stack on a plate.

Icing

8 oz (225 g)/1 cup sugar
6 fl oz (170 ml)/¾ cup water
4 oz (110 g) chocolate
brandy to taste

Dissolve the sugar in the water and bring to the boil. Boil for 3 minutes to make a syrup.
Melt the chocolate, then add enough syrup to make a creamy consistency. Add a *little* brandy to taste. Pour over the profiteroles.

Hunter's Hotel

THERE IS A PHOTOGRAPH in the bar of this old Coach House Inn (now Hunter's Hotel) of Ireland's first motor car. The motor car was to supersede the coaches and chases on which the inn had built up its considerable reputation. Lesser establishments of the same genre closed their doors with the advent of this new phenomenon, not so Mr Hunter's. His descendants over the next decades were to introduce innovations like bedrooms with bathrooms en suite, and to build on his reputation for comfort and superb food.

Time was when ladies and gentlemen would descend from their carriages to enjoy afternoon tea in the carefully manicured formal gardens or under the magnolia tree. These amenities, which have drawn visitors through the centuries, are still there, but Hunter's Hotel no longer caters for the traveller who wants to change horses!

Hunter's Hotel, Rathnew, Co. Wicklow.
Tel: 0404-40106.

Proprietor: Mrs Maureen Gelletlie
Open all year.
How to find
Take N11 to Rathnew village. Turn left just before village on Dublin side.
Restaurant
Dinner IR£16.00 from 7.30 to 9.00 pm.
Lunch 1.00 to 3.00 pm.
Afternoon tea IR£3.50.
No service charge.
Accommodation
Bed and breakfast with bath IR£27.50 per person.
No. of bedrooms: 17
American Express, Visa, Access and Diners credit cards accepted.
French spoken.

The oldest part of the coach house dates back to 1720. The inn is recorded in guide books during the 18th and 19th centuries, so it would seem to predate the motor car by nearly 200 years. Visitors' books for most of this century and some of the last still exist. The gardens on the banks of the Vartry River won the Irish Gardens Award in 1980.

Grilled Oysters

This dish is perfectly suited to the larger oysters now being farmed on the Irish coastline.

24 oysters in the half shell
2 oz (55 g)/¼ cup butter
2 teaspoon Worcestershire sauce
salt and freshly ground pepper

Garnish

6 wedges of lemon
brown bread and butter

Open the oysters, detach from their shells and put onto a grill pan. In a small saucepan melt the butter, add the Worcestershire sauce and pour a spoonful over each oyster. Season and put under a hot grill until the oysters begin to curl at the edges. Serve at once with lemon wedges and brown bread and butter.

Stuffed Goose

To make traditional brown gravy it is a good idea to pour a glass of port over the goose before the end of cooking time. This, with the juices from the pan will give strength to the sauce.

One 7-8 lb (3-3½ kilo) goose.

For the stuffing

2 medium onions
1 tablespoon sage
4 cups breadcrumbs
salt and black pepper
a little lemon juice

Preheat the oven to 350°F/180°C/Regulo 4.

To prepare the stuffing: sweat the onions in a little bacon fat, stir in the sage. Add the breadcrumbs, salt and pepper. If it is too dry, moisten with a little stock or water. Singe and clean the goose and spoon the stuffing into the crop. Place any excess stuffing into the carcase. Rub with salt, pepper and lemon juice. Roast 2-2½ hours. Baste often. Serve with baked roast parsnips and creamed potatoes.

Apricot Mousse

This is a delicious sweet, and the toasted almond slivers scattered over the dish make a nice finish.

8 oz (225 g) dried apricots, soaked overnight
pared rind and juice of ½ lemon
2 medium apples, peeled, cored and sliced
sugar to taste
whites of 2-3 eggs
2 ozs (55 g)/½ cup toasted almonds

Stew the apricots gently with lemon rind, juice and apples. Drain off the juice and rub through a sieve or strainer. When cold, sweeten the purée, and continue to whisk until well mixed. Pile into individual glasses and top with the toasted almonds.

Tinakilly House

FOUR-POSTER BEDS, LOG FIRES and period furniture make this a warm mature hotel for those who like peace and quiet. A seafarer's home par excellence, from the odd porthole window with a view of the sea to the majestic bathroom (happily kept intact) with its giant mahogany-mounted bath, marble basin and throne-like loo, in all their Victorian glory, in front of a roaring fire. Stately reception rooms invite you to contemplate, congregate or just sit and sip your port after dinner in splendid unseaman-like comfort. Bee and William Power have certainly earned full marks for furnishing and decorating the house in correct Victorian style.

Tinakilly House Hotel,
Rathnew, Co. Wicklow.
Tel: 0404-69274 or 67227. Fax: 0404-67806.

Reservations: U.S.A. Robert Reid Associates 800-223-6510 or Selective 800-233-6764 or 800-522-5568.
Proprietors: William and Bee Power
Open all year.
How to find
Take the N11 to Rathnew village, then the R750 towards Wicklow town. The entrance is on the left, 500 metres from the village.
Restaurant
Dinner from IR£23.00 from 7.30 to 9.00 pm.
10% service charge.
Accommodation
Bed and breakfast incl. full Irish breakfast from £35.00-£50.00 (per person sharing).
*No. of bedrooms:*13.   *No. of suites:* 1.
All major credit cards accepted.
English, Irish and French spoken.

Tinakilly House was built in 1870 for Captain Halpin who laid the
first telegraph cable across the Atlantic as Commander of the
'Great Eastern'. His architect was James Franklin Fuller and it is
one of his best works. The most imposing space is the double height
staircase hall designed as a central living room.

Chicken or Game Consommé

2 lb (900 g) chicken (or game) carcases and giblets
2 lb (900 g) vegetables: carrots, turnip, parsnip, leek, etc.
sprig thyme
2 bay leaves
salt and pepper

Break down the carcases in a large saucepan, add the giblets and just cover with water. Simmer gently (the water should barely move) for 3½ hours, add the vegetables and herbs and simmer for 1 hour. Sieve, skim off any excess fat and then filter through muslin. Season.

Lamb in a Basil Sauce 'aux petits légumes'

1 leg lamb
2 tablespoons olive oil and 5 oz (140 g)/⅝ cup butter
salt and pepper
2-3 sprigs basil
2 shallots
3 carrots
3 turnips
2 tablespoons white wine
1 pint (600 ml)/2½ cups veal stock
4 fl oz (125 ml)/¼ cup mushroom juice
parsley

Fry lamb in a pan in the oil and ½ oz (15 g)/1 tablespoon of the butter. Season with salt, pepper and 1 teaspoon of finely chopped basil. Place on a rectangle of tin foil large enough to wrap the joint. Bake until cooked through, approx. 1½-2 hours at 400°F/200°C/Regulo 6. Meanwhile cut shallots, carrots and turnips into the size of large olives and fry in the pan in the same oil and butter, provided it is not burnt. Add a drop of white wine and more fresh basil and reduce. Add veal stock and mushroom juice. Reduce again by half. Enrich with some more butter. When the lamb is cooked, place on its serving dish and decorate with parsley. Serve the sauce separately.

Individually Cooked Apple Tarts

Take one eating apple (per person). Peel and core. Slice at base so the apple will sit firmly, maintaining the apple shape. Insert a marzipan finger in place of core. Place on a 3 inch (8 cm) diameter, ¼ inch (6 mm) thick, circle of shortcrust pastry. Cook at 400 °F/200 °C/Regulo 6 for 20 minutes. Dust over with dry icing sugar and serve on a large plate with mango and raspberry coulis.

Mango and Raspberry Coulis

Liquidise the fruit and strain out pips. Sweeten the purée to taste. Mangoes must be peeled and stoned.

The Old Rectory

LINDA AND PAUL SAUNDERS run the lovely Old Rectory hotel/restaurant in its tranquil garden setting just outside the harbour town of Wicklow. It has a small, pleasant restaurant, candle-lit, and in the cooler evenings, a great log fire. Not surprisingly, as the Old Rectory is situated near the sea, fish is a specialty and is served, as is all the food, with great individuality. Salmon, lobster, crab and sea trout are fresh from the sea. There are other interesting things, like chicken with cream cheese and grapes in puff pastry, on the menu and to finish off you can have 'Swan Lake', the result of Linda's wizardry with the piping bag.

Bedrooms are colourful, tastefully furnished and well equipped. You can choose an Irish, Swiss, or Scottish breakfast to start your day. County Wicklow, one of the loveliest counties in Ireland is waiting outside to be explored.

The Old Rectory,
Wicklow, Co. Wicklow.
Tel: 0404-67048

Reservations: In U.S. call Toll Free 800-223-6510.
In U.K. dial 010-353-404-67048.
Proprietors: Paul and Linda Saunders.
Open 13 April to 14 October.

How to find
1½km off Route N11 on Dublin edge of Wicklow town. ½ km from Wicklow Railway Station. Dublin Airport 55 km. Dun Laoghaire 35km.

Restaurant
Dinner at 8 pm, table d'hôte menu IR£20
À la carte IR£18-IR£25.
No service charge.

Accommodation
Bed and breakfast with bath IR£34 per person
2 nights dinner, bed and breakfast from IR£92.
All major credit cards accepted.
No. of bedrooms: 5.

This ex-rectory was built in 1875 and has been converted into a
small hotel/restaurant. The style is Victorian, typical of the
domestic architecture of Irish country rectories, with marble
fireplaces, white in the lounge and black in the dining room, a
customary arrangement for old rectories – wedding parties
to one room and funeral parties to another!

Potato and Ham Soup

2 pints (1.150 litres)/5 cups ham stock, (not too salty)
1 lb (450 g)/3 cups potatoes, peeled and chopped roughly
1 large onion, peeled and chopped roughly
4 bay leaves
2 tablespoons cooked ham, chopped
1 tablespoon fresh chives or spring onion tops, chopped
salt and freshly ground black pepper
2 oz (55 g)/¼ cup cream
Nutmeg

Bring the first four ingredients to the boil and simmer until the potatoes are tender.Remove bay leaves and liquidise until smooth. Bring back to the boil and simmer for 2 minutes. Add the chopped ham and chives; adjust the seasoning according to your taste. (If a slightly richer taste is desired, stir in one teaspoon of brandy and one teaspoon of butter.) Serve in warmed soup bowls topped with a teaspoon of whipped cream and a tiny pinch of nutmeg.

Crab Claws Malibu

The mouth-watering sweetness of freshly cooked crab claws makes us wonder why lobster is so highly thought of. We use the claws of Kilmore Quay crabs and crack all of the outside shell, except the pincer, to make them easier to eat. Enthusiastic diners will inevitably finish up by dipping the claws in the delicious sauce with their finger, so provide a finger bowl of lukewarm water with thin slices of lemon floating on top.

36 large cooked crab claws, with shell removed
1 pint (600 ml)/2½ cups well-flavoured fish stock
1 oz (30 g)/¼ cup dessicated coconut
3 oz (85 g)/6 tablespoons butter
2 oz (55 g)/¾ cup flour
4 oz (110 g)/1¼ cups button mushrooms, washed and quartered
4 oz (110 g)/⅔ cup diced fresh pineapple
4 fl oz (120 ml)/½ cup double cream
2 fl oz (60 ml)/¼ cup Malibu coconut liqueur
salt and cayenne pepper

Place crab claws in one layer in buttered ovenproof serving dish. Dot with 1 oz (30 g)/2 tablespoons butter, cover with foil and heat through at 300 °F/150 °C/Regulo 2 for 25 minutes. Melt 2 oz (55 g)/4 tablespoons butter in a pan, blend in flour, cook over low heat for 2-3 minutes, stirring constantly with a wooden spoon. Add the warmed fish stock gradually, beating all the time so that the sauce stays smooth, and bring to the boil. Simmer for 5 minutes. Add coconut, mushrooms, pineapple and cream. Heat through, but do not boil. Add salt and a pinch of cayenne pepper to taste. Finally, blend in the coconut liqueur and pour immediately over the crab claws. Toss gently to coat all claws in sauce and incorporate any spare butter.

To serve: Decorate with trimmed pineapple leaves and cucumber 'fans'. Green vegetables or a salad make a good accompaniment.

'Swan Lake' meringues

We were looking for a memorable and beautiful shape in which to pipe meringues (having previously made baskets, shamrocks and baroque shapes), when I read the Irish folk tale *The Singing Swans*. These meringues are the result. Our diners are so thrilled when they see them that they have often rushed for their cameras to take photographs! The basic meringue shapes are made in advance and assembled just before serving. They are a bit fragile to handle but well worth the effort. Any colours may be used but we find this combination of pale pink meringue and fresh green fruit particularly pleasing.

Whisk 4 egg whites until stiff and dry. Add 4 oz (110 g)/½ cup granulated sugar and whisk at full speed for 30 seconds. Add 4 oz (110 g)/½ cup sieved castor sugar and whisk only until combined. Add 2 drops peppermint essence and 1 drop red food colouring, whisking lightly until just blended in. (N.B. Use a spoon, not the bottle.) Take 3 flat baking trays, 16 inch by 12 inch (30.5 cm by 40.5 cm), cover in aluminium foil, then lightly grease all three. Using a piping bag and a star nozzle pipe 8 'bases', 16 'wings', and (on the foil covered tray), 10 'necks' (i.e. 8 plus 2 for breakages) as shown. (If you have any spare mixture make a few stars and sprinkle with cocoa powder or stud with flaked almonds for *petit fours* on a future occasion.) Bake for 3 hours at 150 °F/70 °C/Regulo ⅛. When cooked, remove trays from oven, release 'necks' by peeling away

foil (very carefully indeed) and release 'bases' and 'wings' by gently flexing trays. When cool, store in an airtight box (for up to 3
months). If any of the shapes begin to break, keep the pieces. They
can be invisibly mended with a dab of cream at time of assembly.

To serve: Whip ½ pint (300 ml)/1¼ cups cream until stiff. Stick
'base' to serving plate with a dab of cream, place a heaped tablespoon of cream on top, stick 'wings' one each side and 'neck' into
the cream, centre front. Arrange green fruits, e.g. sliced kiwi fruits
or halved, de-seeded green grapes around the swan to represent
the lake, and fill back of swan with soft fruits such as strawberries
or prepared pieces of chocolate. The final effect is enhanced by a
small fresh flower and a larger sized under-plate covered with a
doyley.

pipe 8 'bases'

16 'wings'

10 'necks'
(on the foil covered tray)

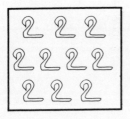

assemble like this:

Rathsallagh House –'not a hotel'

THIS VERY UNUSUAL 200-YEAR-OLD FARM HOUSE, surrounded by 500 acres of parkland and a working farm, is approached by a mile-long driveway. The two-storey stretch of house blends nonchalantly into its environment and is entered through an arch leading into a picturesque 19th-century courtyard. The house extends around the courtyard. Once inside the 'non-hotel' you realise you are in a house of infinite charm. This is no luxury hotel but rather a country house – roomy, comfortable, warm and never stuffy, with many areas to sit in comfort.

The old farmhouse kitchen is a gem. The ten bedrooms are all very *House and Garden* chic and all very big (one is called the 'half acre'). By hotel standards the adjoining bathrooms are massive. Everywhere there are big windows with views of the park and gardens. Some of the bedrooms open directly onto the great restored walled garden.

Joe and Kay O'Flynn took over the house ten years ago. They are both well-known in local 'horsey' circles and can organise horses for guests wishing to ride. There are friendly dogs, placid and charming as only much-loved dogs can be.

Kay is the *chef de cuisine* and with Joan Purcell controls the sophisticated menu using mainly local produce supplemented by vegetables and herbs fresh from the garden.

Although not compulsory, you can hunt, shoot, play tennis, golf, swim or play billiards without leaving the estate or you can just watch your fellow guests be energetic while you let your own cobwebs blow away. A first visit could easily be the start of a love affair with this very charming place.

Rathsallagh House, Dunlavin, Co. Wicklow.

Tel: 045-53112. Fax: 045-53343.
Reservations: Robert Reid Associates.
Proprietors: Joe and Kay O'Flynn.
Open all year, except Christmas and New Year.

How to find
2 miles Dunlavin. 15 miles Naas or Curragh. 35 miles Dublin.

Restaurant
Lunch from IR£19.80 (Sunday only, 2.30 pm).
Dinner from IR£21.45 (8-9 pm).
No service charge. VAT included.

Accommodation
Bed and breakfast from IR£46 p.p. sharing.
Double let as single from IR£57.50.
No. of bedrooms: 10.
Credit cards: Visa, Access, Diners. *German spoken.*

*The original house was burnt down during the 1798
'Troubles'. The owners never got around to restoring the house.
They moved into the stables and turned the boxes into living
rooms and the hayloft into bedrooms. The present owners went
even further, giving it the finishing touches which make
Rathsallagh House and gardens what it is today.*

Oysters with Quail Eggs and Sour Cream Dressing

18 oysters
18 quail eggs, poached

Dressing

12 fl oz (370 ml)/1½ cups sour cream
2 tablespoons spring onions, chopped
1 teaspoon Worcestershire sauce
juice of ½ lemon
salt and cayenne pepper

Garnish

chopped chives
lettuce leaves
1 hard boiled egg yolk sieved

Mix dressing ingredients together. Make a bed of lettuce on six plates. Put three quail eggs on each plate; top with a little dressing. Arrange three oysters in their shells on the lettuce. Sprinkle with chopped chives and sieved yolk.

Pork Fillets Stuffed with Prunes

2 pork fillets
juice of 1 lemon or lime
½ pint (300 ml)/1¼ cups boiling water
8 oz (225 g) dried prunes

Stuffing

1 lb (450 g) sausage meat
1 clove garlic, crushed
8 juniper berries, crushed
handful of chopped chives, crushed
handful chopped parsley
3 tablespoons dry white wine
1 large apple, diced
walnut halves
Garnish: fried apple slices

Pour boiling water over the prunes and lemon juice and leave for 3-4 hours. Drain and remove stones. Trim the pork and slit to flatten open.

Stuffing

Mix the sausage meat, garlic, juniper berries, chives, parsley, wine and apples. Season. Arrange one-third of the prunes on each pork fillet and place the walnuts between them. Divide the stuffing between the two and spread evenly. Arrange the remaining prunes on one of the fillets and cover with the other, meat-side up. Roast in a moderate oven, 350°F/180°C/Regulo 4 for 45-50 minutes until cooked through.

Slice thinly to serve and arrange with fried apple slices on each plate.

Autumn Pudding

Note: It is difficult to give quantities – you can adjust them to the bowl size and the combination of fruits you want to use.

lightly cooked dessert apples
blackberries
redcurrants
dried apricots
5 fl oz (150 ml)/ ⅝ cup orange juice
fresh apple, chopped
lightly cooked chopped pears
chopped plums, stoned
slices of stale white bread
sugar to taste

Soak the apricots for 3-4 hours.
In a large pan combine all the fruits and juice. Bring gently to a simmer and cook slowly until the apricots are soft. Sweeten to taste.
Dip the bread in the juices and use to line a pudding basin. Pour in the fruit and top with another slice of bread. Cover with cling wrap and leave in the fridge with a weight on top for 24 hours.
Serve chilled with a jug of cream.

Doyle's Schoolhouse Restaurant

JOHN DOYLE, AN ENTHUSIASTIC COOK, returned from 'foreign parts' to his own village to start Doyle's Schoolhouse Restaurant in 1975. The sophisticated menu contains many Irish favourites. It has great local appeal but sadly it is often missed by tourists.

Doyle's Schoolhouse Restaurant,
Castledermot, Co. Kildare.
Tel: 0503-44282. Fax: c/o 0503-43653.

Proprietor: Doyle family.
Open all year.
Children welcome.
How to find
On main Waterford/Dublin road N9. Village of Castledermot.
Restaurant
Wine bar. Lunch IR£5.
Dinner from IR£17.00, 6.30-10.30 pm summer, 7.30.-10.00 pm winter.
Sunday lunch 12.30-2.00 pm.
No service charge.
All major credit cards accepted.

An interesting example of an Irish village school now remodelled principally as restaurant but with four bedrooms with en suite bathrooms upstairs. The village of great historical interest with its round tower, Celtic crosses, and Norman arch. The remains of St John's Friary, at one time a noted leper hospital, are across the road from the restaurant. The most recent historical treasure (unearthed in 196? is a Viking stone known as a Hogback, the only known one in Ireland.

Lambs' Brains Schoolhouse Style

6 sets lambs' brains

Batter
4 oz (110 g)/1 cup flour
1 oz (30 g)/2 tablespoon butter
1 tablespoon brandy
2 egg whites
salt, pepper
warm water

Sauce
8 hard-boiled egg yolks
13 fl oz (400 ml)/1⅝ cup olive oil
juice of 1 lemon
2 teaspoons capers (chopped)
salt and pepper

Prepare the batter by melting the butter and adding it with enough warm water to the flour to make it the texture of heavy cream. Mix in the brandy. Season and fold in the egg whites. Rest for 1 hour. Slice the brains into medallions. Dip into the batter and deep fry until golden brown.

Sauce
Blend the yolks and lemon juice in a liquidiser, add a little oil and blend until emulsified. Incorporate all the oil. Stir in the capers.

Pigeon Breast with Lime and Peppery Pineapple

Ingredients per person:
4 pigeon breasts
4 small tomatoes (optional)
watercress leaves (optional)
butter for cooking

Sauce

34 fl oz (1.060 l) pigeon stock
5½ oz (155 g)/⅝ cup granulated sugar
5 fl oz (160 ml)/⅝ cup white vinegar
juice of 4 limes
salt and pepper

Pineapple

2 pineapple slices
6½ tablespoons white wine vinegar
3½ tablespoons red wine vinegar
6 tablespoons granulated sugar
2 tablespoons whole peppercorns

Candied zest

zest of 4 limes
zest of 4 lemons
equal amounts of sugar and water

Sauce

Place the vinegar and sugar in a small saucepan. Boil until the mixture begins to caramelise. Add the lime juice and cook 10 minutes, then add the pigeon stock and cook slowly, uncovered for at least one hour to reduce. Season with salt and pepper as needed. Reserve. Remove the pineapple rind and any hard spots in the pulp. Cut the pineapple in half lengthwise, then halve each piece lengthwise. Remove the central core. Save any juice that comes from the fruit. Cut into large chunks. Place both vinegars, peppercorns and sugar in a saucepan and simmer for 30 minutes. Add the pineapple and continue cooking for 20 minutes. Remove from heat and set aside. Cut the lime and orange zest into julienne strips. Make a sugar syrup by bringing the sugar and water to the boil without stirring. Cook the strips in the syrup until softened and they have become candied. Set aside. Heat a little butter in a frying pan and cook the pigeon breasts over low heat for 12-15 minutes (they should only be rare).

To serve: Spoon some sauce onto each plate. Slice the pigeon breasts and place on top of the sauce. Spoon a little sauce over the meat, then sprinkle the candied zest over it. Place some of the pineapple on each plate and decorate (if desired) with a tomato cut like a flower on some fresh watercress leaves, and serve.

Walnut and Almond Gâteau

12 oz (340 g)/1½ cups sugar
7 eggs
4 oz (110 g)/1 cup walnuts, chopped
4 oz (110 g)/½ cup almonds, ground
1 teaspoon vanilla extract
3 oz (85 g)/¾ cup cornflour
10 fl oz (300 ml)/1¼ cups whipped cream, sweetened
6½ oz (200 ml) coffee flavoured crème anglaise

Mix together the sugar, 1 whole egg and 6 egg yolks. Beat well so that a smooth paste is obtained. Add the walnuts, ground almonds, vanilla and cornflour. Gently incorporate the stiffly beaten egg-whites with the other ingredients. Pour into a buttered and floured cake tin. Bake in a moderate oven for 35 minutes. Let cool and cut into layers. Spread each layer with whipped cream. Place the layers on top of each other and coat the top with the coffee-flavoured crème anglaise.

Marlfield House

'A very agreeable place'

THOSE WHO LOVE THE OLD AND MATURE will appreciate Marlfield House. Furniture and decoration are perfect. The bedrooms are spacious and elegant. The food is plentiful and expertly cooked. The former 23,150 acre estate has shrunk to 35 acres. A previous visitor (in 1776) wrote this description of the landscape which is quite fitting today:

'Courtown is an agreeable place, and in some respects a very singular one, for the house is within 600 yards of the sea, and yet is almost buried in fine woods which from their growth and foliage show no aversion to their neighbours, who is so often pernicious to all their brethren. His (Lord Courtown's) views of the sea are fine, everywhere broken by wood or hilly varied ground. All his environs consist of undulating lands, which give a pleasant variety to the scene; a river enters his garden, and pursuing for some distance a sequested course, shaded on one side by a rocky bank, well wooded, and on the other by lofty trees, with a very agreeable walk under them, pours itself into the sea at a small distance from the house.'

Marlfield House Hotel,
Gorey, Co. Wexford.
Tel: 055-21124. Fax: 055-21572. Telex 80757.
Reservations: Telephone, telex or fax Robert Reid Associates, 800-223-6510.
Selective Hotel Reservations, Inc., 800-223-6764 or 800-522-5568 (Toll Free)
N.Y. State. N.Y. City.
Proprietors: Ray and Mary Bowe.
Open all year except 2 weeks January.

How to find
2 km from Gorey on Courtown Road.

Restaurant
Lunch 1.00-2.30 pm from IR£14.50.
Dinner 7.30-9.30 pm from IR£26.
10% service charge.

Accommodation
Bed and breakfast from IR£55.
No. of bedrooms: 13. *No. of suites:* 6.
All major credit cards accepted.
French and German spoken.

Two mansions existed originally on the Courtown estate –
Courtown House and its Dower House (Marlfield today). The former was
the grander house with an estate of 23,150 acres which supported a
lifestyle of great luxury and entertainment on a grand scale. Following the
Irish famine of 1845-1849, when rent revenue dropped appreciably, like
many of the mansions of its day, Courtown became very dilapidated and
was eventually demolished in 1948. The Dower House (Marlfield) became
the principal residence in Ireland of the Courtowns until it was
acquired by the Bowe family in 1979.

Salade de Pigeon

    walnut vinaigrette
    2 pigeon breasts (marinated overnight in: olive oil, garlic,
    orange zest, shallot, black pepper)
    curly endive
    raddichio lettuce
    oak leaf lettuce
    fine, crispy garlic croûtons
    2 oz (55 g)/2 rashers of bacon
    finely sliced white mushrooms

Make a salad of the three types of lettuce, gently coated in the vinai-
grette, alternating the colours of leaves. In a pan, sauté the seasoned pigeon breasts for about 4 minutes. Remove from heat and
allow to relax. Fry the bacon and mushrooms quickly in hot fat
until crispy. Add to dish with pigeon breasts. Allow to absorb pigeon juices; then sprinkle bacon and mushrooms on salad. Finely
carve the pink breasts and arrange attractively on the salad.
Sprinkle with a few croûtons and serve immediately.

Darne de Saumon aux Pointes d'Asperges

    12 spears of asparagus
    3 tablespoons fresh chervil
    2 middle-cut steaks of wild salmon
    fish stock
    ½ oz (15 ml)/cream
    1 oz (30 g)/2 tablespoons butter
    chives, finely chopped

Place the prepared asparagus in enough boiling seasoned water to
cover. Add some fresh chervil and a knob of butter. Cook for 20
minutes or until tender. Place the salmon in a shallow pan of boiling fish stock. Cover and place in a moderate oven and cook for 7-8
minutes or until just cooked. Remove the fish and keep warm. Boil
the liquid until only 2 tablespoons remain. Add cream and butter
and beat vigorously to bind the sauce. Add the chives at the last
moment. Arrange the asparagus on the plate with the salmon. Coat
with the warm sauce. Serve immediately.

Tarte au Citron

1 quantity from recipe for shortbread dough
14 oz (370 g) /1¾ cups castor sugar
pinch flour
10 fl oz (300 ml)/1¼ cups cream
4 lemons
9 eggs

To make shortbread

8 oz (225 g)/1 cup butter
4 oz (110 g)/¾ cup icing sugar
2 egg yolks
10 oz (285 g)/1¼ cups flour
pinch salt
drop of vanilla or lemon essence

Cut the butter into short pieces and place it on a wooden surface. Work the butter with your fingertips until it is very soft. Sift the icing sugar and add it to the butter with a pinch of salt. Work the mixture, still with fingertips, until the ingredients are thoroughly blended, then add the egg yolks and lightly mix all the ingredients together. Sift the flour and using your right hand amalgamate it evenly into the mixture. When the pastry is thoroughly mixed, add the vanilla or lemon essence. Rub the pastry two or three times, using the palm of your hand, but do not over-work it. Roll it into a ball and flatten it out lightly. Wrap in greaseproof paper and chill for several hours.

Pre-heat oven to 325 °F/160 °C/Regulo 3. On a lightly floured wooden surface, roll out the shortbread pastry to about ⅙ inch (4 mm) thick. Butter a flan ring 9 inches (25 cm) diameter, 1½ inches (4 cm) deep. Place on a buttered baking sheet and line with the pastry. Put a circle of greaseproof paper in the bottom, fill with dried beans and bake in preheated oven for 10 minutes. Remove from the oven, take out the beans and paper and keep the pastry shell at room temperature. Lower the oven temperature to 300 °F(150 °C)/Regulo 2.

Lemons
Wash, grate the zests and squeeze the lemons, reserving the zests and juice together.

Eggs
Break them into a bowl, add the sugar and beat lightly with a wire whisk until the mixture is smooth and well blended.

Cream
Pour the cream onto the egg mixture and beat very lightly with a wire whisk. Stir in the lemon juice and zests and pour the filling onto the pastry case.

Cooking
Place immediately in the pre-heated oven and cook for 40 minutes. If the top of the tart becomes too brown before the end of the cooking time, cover with foil. When the tart is cooked, remove the flan ring before it cools completely.

Step House Restaurant

THE DESCENDANTS OF THE MACMURRAGH KAVANAGHS still live in Borris. One of the more famous members of the family in the last century was Arthur who, though born limbless, learned to ride, fish, shoot and sail. He travelled alone to Egypt, Scandinavia, Russia and India. He had a sojourn to the Palace of Westminster as M.P. for Carlow for 12 years. He also married and had children. He was ill in Persia and nursed back to health in the harem of a Persian prince. Arthur's daughter Agnes died at the Step House in the Autumn of 1930. The Coady family purchased the house after Agnes's death and turned it into a restaurant. With such a history I expected a warm and interesting place with charm and personality and it certainly lived up to my expectations. The food and wine were excellent.

Step House Restaurant,
Borris, Co. Carlow.
Tel: 0503-73401. Fax: 0503-73395.

Proprietor: Breda Coady
Closed 1-28 February and every Monday except bank holidays.

How to find
Dublin: 72 miles. Rosslare: 35 miles. Kilkenny and Carlow: 16 miles.

Restaurant
Gourmet table d'hôte from IR£17.90. Served 7.00-9.00 pm.
Bistro – light meals from IR£5.90.
Open for lunch and dinner.
Sunday lunch speciality.

Accommodation
No. of bedrooms: 6.
Visa card accepted.

Amenities
Championship golf courses in nearby Carlow
and Mount Juliet Country Club.

The Step House was formerly part of the estate of the MacMurragh Kavanaghs – once Kings of Leinster – opposite which it is sited. It is thought to have been built by the architect William Morrison c.1820. A Gothic front door gives access to Greek Revival Interior and the windows overlook the imposing entrance gates of the estate.

Artichauts Farci

4-6 artichokes
4 oz (110 g)/1 cup crab meat
4 oz (110 g)/1 cup prawns

Dressing

½ or 1 small green pepper, chopped
10 fl oz (300 ml)/½ pint mayonnaise flavoured with grated
lemon rind
2 tablespoons snipped chives and parsley or spring onion
salt
ground black pepper

Trim off the points of the leaves of the artichokes with scissors and trim the stalk from the bottom. Cook the artichokes in boiling salted water until a leaf can be pulled out, about 35-40 minutes. Drain, refresh and leave until cold. Meanwhile, prepare the dressing. Drop the green pepper into boiling water, cook for 1 minute, then drain and dry. Mix the mayonnaise with lemon juice and sugar. Add the green pepper and herbs or spring onion to the dressing. Pull out the centre leaves from each artichoke and scrape away the 'choke'. Mix the flaked crab meat with the prawns and moisten with the dressing. Put a spoonful of the crab mixture in the centre of each artichoke. Serve cold.

Chicken Valencia with Pine Nuts

4 large chicken breasts, split lengthwise and beaten flat
seasoned flour
2 tablespoons oil
1 tablespoon butter
4 fl oz (120 ml)/½ cup Cointreau
2 oranges
4 teaspoons Dijon mustard
3 tablespoons cultured sour cream
1 teaspoon thyme
2 fl oz (60 ml)/¼ cup chicken stock
sea salt and freshly ground black pepper
2 dessertspoons pine nuts, lightly toasted

Toss chicken in seasoned flour. Put oil and butter in a heavy pan, and when very hot add the chicken, reduce heat and lightly brown for 2-4 minutes each side (depending on the thickness). Discard the fat in the pan, remove the chicken and keep warm. Retain any sediment in the pan and add the liquor. Flame and reduce to a syrup – do not allow the pan to overheat at this stage. Add mustard, sour cream, thyme, 2 teaspoons finely grated orange rind, salt and pepper. Return pan to low heat with chicken and stock. Cook for 2-5 minutes. Arrange on a plate with nuts tossed on top and garnish with the peeled orange slices. Serve with new potatoes.

Framboise

6 oz (170 g) rich shortcrust pastry

1 lb (450 g) fresh or frozen raspberries

3 egg whites

6 oz (170 g)/¾ cup sugar

3 oz (85 g)/⅔ cup almonds, (freshly blanched and ground, but not oiled)

1 tablespoon flaked almonds

Line 10 inch (25 cm) flan ring with the pastry. Bake blind (if using fresh raspberries) for about 15 minutes (this is not necessary if using still frozen raspberries). Whisk the egg whites until stiff but not dry, then add 1 tablespoon of measured sugar and whisk for one minute. Cut and fold in the remaining sugar and ground almonds. Fill the flan with the raspberries and top with the meringue mixture making sure to cover all the fruit. Toss the flaked almonds on top. Bake at 350°F/180°C/Regulo 4 for 30-40 minutes. If meringue starts to brown, reduce heat; it shouldn't be any darker than a very light biscuit colour. Serve straight from oven with lightly whipped fresh cream.

Aherne's Seafood Bar

OUTSIDE, AHERNE'S IS A VINTAGE IRISH PUB. Inside it is a world-class seafood bar and restaurant. Situated in the seaport town of Youghal (pronounced 'Yawl') it is run by Gerry Fitzgibbon, his wife Betty and their sons John and David. It started as a bar, serving bar food, and grew in stature and dimension to become locally and internationally acclaimed. The *Los Angeles Times* called it ecstatically 'One of the best seafood restaurants in the world'. Food is still served in the bar as well as in the newly added restaurant. One thing is guaranteed – whichever one you choose, your meal will be a long remembered pleasure.

Aherne's Seafood Bar,
163 North Main Street, Youghal, Co. Cork.
Tel: 024-92424/92533

Proprietor: Owned and managed by Fitzgibbon family
Chef: David Fitzgibbon
Open all year.
Closed all day Monday (except July and August).
Closed Good Friday and 4 days at Christmas.
Children over 8 years only in restaurant.
How to find
On the N25 (main Moscow to Dingle Road!)
Restaurant
Table d'hôte lunch and à la carte Tues.-Sat. 12.30-2.15 from IR£10.50.
Dinner à la carte Tuesday-Sunday 6.30-9.30 pm from IR£15.00.
10% service charge.
All major credit cards accepted.
Extensive menu served all day in cocktail bar.

*An 18th century pub and grocery store converted into a
restaurant in 1969 and extended in 1984. Near the great church of
St Mary's and some of the oldest houses in Ireland.*

Aherne's Hot Potato and Smoked Salmon Starter

1½ oz (45 g)/3 tablespoons garlic butter
6 medium-sized cooked potatoes
6 oz (170 g) sliced, smoked salmon
6 oz (170 g)/1⅓ cups grated cheese
½ pint (300 ml)/1¼ cups cream
freshly ground black pepper
salt
juice of 1 lemon

Grease six 3 inch (7.5 cm) ramekin dishes with garlic butter. Thinly slice cold potato and layer the bottom of the dish. Place the smoked salmon on top and season with black pepper and lemon juice. Put another layer of potato on top and cover with grated cheese. Pour cream over and bake in a hot oven for 10 minutes or until nicely browned. Garnish with a sprig of parsley.

Sea Bass Baked in Orange Juice and White Wine

Six 6 oz (170 g) fillets of sea bass
juice of 10 oranges
⅓ bottle dry white wine
6 bay leaves
6 sprigs of fennel
olive oil

Coat 6 flat ovenproof dishes with olive oil. Place a fillet of fish in each dish and season with freshly ground black pepper. Pour over orange juice and wine and add a bay-leaf and sprig of fennel to each dish. Bake in a hot oven for approx. 20 minutes.

Ballymaloe House

BALLYMALOE HOUSE HAS ALWAYS BEEN synonymous with great cooking. In County Cork where international award winning restaurants abound, it is in good company. Much of the food comes from the Allen family farms and the fish from neighbouring fishing villages. The family enterprises also include a craft shop, farm shop and cookery school. The hotel has 30 bedrooms in the main building and courtyard. Ivan Allen is the family wine buff and Myrtle is responsible for the wizardry in the kitchen. A benign ghost called Chuff (a dwarf) is said to haunt the old castle but he doesn't seem to ruffle the tranquility of Ballymaloe House in Shanagarry.

Ballymaloe House,
Shanagarry, Midleton, Co. Cork.
Tel: 021-652531. Fax: 021-652021. Telex: 75028

Reservations: Robert Reid Associates, telephone 800-223-6510 or direct.
Proprietors: Ivan and Myrtle Allen.
Closed Christmas for 3 days.
Children welcome.

How to find
The house is situated on the L35, two miles beyond Cloyne, on the Ballycotton road.

Restaurant
Dinner IR£24. Lunch IR£13.
10% service charge.

Accommodation
B and B + bath IR£38 to IR£42.
No. of bedrooms: 30.

The history of the original castle (of which part remains) dates back to 1450. Built by the Fitzgerald family it was held by them until 1641, when it passed to Lord Broghill who entertained both William Penn and Cromwell at Ballymaloe. Changing hands many times during the 17th, 18th and 19th centuries, it passed to Ivan Allen in 1948 and became an hotel in 1967.

Lettuce and Mint Soup

4 oz (110 g)/1 cup peeled diced onions

5 oz (140 g)/1 cup chopped potatoes

1 teaspoon salt

freshly-ground pepper

6 oz (170 g)/3 cups chopped lettuce leaves

2 pints (1.2 ltrs)/5 cups stock

2 teaspoons freshly chopped mint

1 tablespoon cream (optional)

2 oz (55 g)/4 tablespoons butter

Melt butter in a heavy saucepan. When it foams, add potatoes and onions and turn them until well coated. Sprinkle with salt and pepper. Cover and sweat on a gentle heat for 10 minutes. Add chopped lettuce leaves and stock. Boil until soft. Liquidise, sieve or put through a mouli. Do not overcook or the vegetables will lose their flavour. Adjust seasoning. Add mint and cream.

Note: Good for using the coarse outer leaves of the lettuce, or a head that is starting to wilt or shoot.

Lamb Roast with Irish Garden Herbs

5 lb (2.25 kilo) joint of lamb

2 tablespoons good quality oil

2 cloves garlic

1 tablespoon each of the following herbs chopped and mixed in even amounts: parsley, thyme, chives,marjoram, mint, tarragon

1 level teaspoon finely chopped rosemary

1 extra teaspoon each of these herbs for the sauce

8 fl oz (250 ml)/1 cup stock

Prepare a paste of the oil, garlic and herbs. Peel and crush garlic in a little salt and blend with the oil. Mix in the chopped herbs. Sprinkle the lamb with salt and pepper and rub in the herb mixture. The lamb can be left to stand in this mixture for up to 24 hours, or can be roasted right away.

Preheat oven to 400°F/200°C/Regulo 6. Roast lamb for approximately 1½ to 1¾ hours, when it should be slightly pink in the middle. Test with a skewer – the juices should run out pink. Remove lamb and place on a warm serving dish. Meanwhile spoon off the surplus fat from the roasting pan. Add the herbs and stock to the cooking juices. Boil up, scraping the pan well and serve separately in a sauce boat.

Irish Mist Soufflé

10-14 lemons

4 eggs

1 large sweet geranium leaf (Pelargonium Gravolens)

1 tablespoon Irish Mist

4 tablespoons castor sugar

2 small lemons

2 teaspoons gelatine

This mixture can be filled into lemon skins or served as a soufflé. If filling lemons, cut the tops off, scoop out the insides and strain. Otherwise squeeze lemons in the ordinary way. Crush the geranium leaf in your hand and put it in the lemon juice. Beat egg yolks with sugar to a thick mousse using an electric mixer or by hand over a saucepan of boiling water. Add Irish Mist and beat again. Put gelatine, 2 teaspoons of lemon juice and 1 tablespoon of water in a pyrex or china bowl. Place this in a saucepan of water, making sure it doesn't touch the base of the saucepan. Bring the water to the boil. Do not stir but let simmer until the gelatine has dissolved. Blend gelatine and remaining strained lemon juice with the mousse. Put the geranium leaf in too, if you think enough flavour has not been extracted. Beat egg whites stiffly and fold in. The sweet should be served semi-frozen.

The soufflé

These quantities make 2 pints (1.2 litres)/5 cups in volume, enough to fill a 1½-pint (900ml) soufflé dish. Greaseproof paper should be tied round the soufflé dish to give it another 2 inches (5 cm) in height. You then over-fill the dish, freeze for 4 hours and remove the paper. Top with a rosette of whipped cream and a large geranium leaf.

The Lemons

Fill lemon skins with the mixture and freeze for 4 hours. You will have lemon pulp left over which can be strained and used for some other purpose.

Longueville House and Presidents' Restaurant

IN THIS GRAND OLD HOUSE, built over two centuries ago and situated in a 500 acre wooded estate, you are surrounded by many of Ireland's beauty spots. The twenty guest bedrooms are all individually decorated in superb period style. The public rooms, too, are very elegant but with warmth and comfort. The restaurant is fully licensed, and the food recommended by many international food guides. Ireland's only vineyard is located on the farm.

The history of Longueville reflects the history of Ireland itself. The lands originally owned by Donough O'Callaghan who fought with Catholic Confederates after the collapse of the 1641 Rebellion, were forfeited to Cromwell. The house was built by the Longfield family who appear to have acquired the property from Purdon, a soldier of Cromwell.

Richard Longfield was created Baron Longueville in 1795 and changed the name of the house to Longueville. William O'Callaghan, whose ancestors were deprived of their land by Cromwell, repurchased it in 1938 and it is now owned and run by Michael and Jane O'Callaghan and their son William.

From the house there is a wonderful view of the Blackwater river and the ruined Dromineen Castle, ancient seat of long past O'Callaghans.

Longueville House and Presidents' Restaurant,
Mallow, Co. Cork.

Tel: 022-47156 – 3 lines. Fax: 022-47459.

Reservations: By telephone, fax or post. For U.S.A. reservations call Robert Reid Associates, 800-223-6510 or 800-424-5500 or Selective 800-223-6764.

Proprietors: Michael, Jane and William O'Callaghan.

Open 1 March to 20 December.

How to find

N72 from Mallow.

Restaurant

Lunch IR£14.00. Dinner IR£26.50.

Accommodation

Bed and full Irish breakfast IR£40-60.

No. of bedrooms: 16.

All major credit cards accepted.

French and Irish spoken.

Longueville. Original house was built in 1720 and retained as a centre piece when two wings were added in 1800. The exotic conservatory was added in 1866. The Regency plasterwork ceiling is by an Italian artist.

Game Terrine with Gooseberry Chutney

    1 lb (450 g) minced pork
    2 quail, boned, rolled and browned
    2 oz (55 g) finely chopped onions
    1 clove garlic, crushed
    1 cooking apple, chopped
    1 teaspoon fresh herbs, (e.g. parsley, sage, chives, thyme)
    salt and pepper
    2 oz (55 g) hazelnuts
    1 egg
    ¼ bottle cider

Combine all ingredients together and put into a covered terrine.
Place in a bain-marie and cook in a very low oven (200°F/90°C/Re-
gulo ⅛ for 2-2½ hours. Test, press and leave to cool.

Gooseberry Chutney

    4 lb (1.8 kg) gooseberries
    4 onions
    1 oz (30 g)/1½ tablespoons salt
    1½ lb (675 g/3 cups brown sugar
    ½ lb (225 g)/1½ cups sultanas
    2 pints (1.2 l)/5 cups vinegar
    1 teaspoon dry mustard
    ¼ teaspoon cayenne pepper

Top and tail gooseberries. Chop the onions and put into a greased
saucepan with all the other ingredients. Stir over a low heat until
sugar has completely dissolved. Bring up to the boil, then reduce
heat and simmer until thick and pulpy, stirring frequently. Pour
into sterilised pots and close tightly.

Fillets of Black Sole Rosas

    12 medium fillets of black sole
    24 cooked prawns
    12 blanched spinach or sorrel leaves
    white wine sauce to serve

Fish Cream

½ lb (225 g) trimmings of black sole, prawns or scallops,
3 times ratio cream to fish (approx. 1¼ pint/725 ml)
1 egg white

Gunge up fish trimmings, prawns or scallops in a food processor with the egg white and sieve into a bowl which is over ice (this prevents the mixture cracking). Gradually beat in the cream and season.

Batten out the fish fillets. Spread on a teaspoon of fish cream with a spatula. Blanch the spinach or sorrel leaf and wrap a cooked prawn in it. Place this on the fish cream and add another little bit of cream on top – then fold over the fillet.

Cook for 3-4 minutes in a steamer. Serve with a white wine sauce and decorate with remaining prawns and chervil.

White Wine Sauce

Reduce ½ bottle of medium dry wine with sliced shallots to about one-third of a glass and then add 1 pint/600 ml/2½ cups cream and reduce again to half. Finish by beating in approx 4 oz/110 g/½ cup unsalted butter (away from the direct heat) and finish with a dash of lemon juice and season to taste. Strain.

To serve: Put the sauce on the plate first and then place the two fillets at an angle and decorate with chervil and cooked prawns.

Vanilla Ice Cream with Fresh Fruit in Season

3 egg yolks
4 oz (110 g)/½ cup castor sugar
½ pint (300 ml)/1½ cups cream
few drops vanilla essence

Beat the egg-yolks and sugar together until very creamy. In another bowl, whip the cream until thick. Add the vanilla essence to the yolks and lightly fold in the cream. Transfer to a large plastic container, cover with a lid and freeze until firm.

N.B. Any purée of fresh fruit and sugar can be added to the above to make a flavoured ice-cream. (You will need about ¼ pint (150 ml) good, thick purée, sweetened to taste, for the above quantity.)

Assolas Country House

THE HISTORY OF ASSOLAS FROM 1674-1714 is lost in the mists of time. However, in 1714 it became the property of Rev. Francis Gore who enlarged the estate. Rev. Gore, a man of means and influence, was the rector of Castlemanger Church. In those days a road (still visible today) forded the river beside Assolas House, and legend tells us that Rev. Gore always hung a lantern high on the walls of the house: a welcome light to guide travellers on their way. It is reported that he saved many lives from swollen rivers and from bands of highway men roaming the area. Assolas was always open to receive the wounded, and so well known became his warm and friendly light, that the ford became known in Gaelic as *Atha Solas* (Ford of Light). The Anglicised version has become abbreviated to Assolas. Rev. Gore was a just and humane man at a time when men in his position were feared and disliked. To this day, in Castlemanger church a private pew is reserved for the residents of Assolas as a tribute to him. It is generally accepted that prior to the suppression of the Catholic Church by Queen Elizabeth I, Assolas was occupied by a community of Catholic monks. The present stone outhouses, with still-visible castings of closed-up windows, remind us of its monastic past. Of interest is the Leper's Peep still clearly visible.

Many ancient yew trees in the grounds were planted, in another age, to supply good quality bows to our bow and arrow ancestors.

The house is difficult to locate but ask, ask and ask again; no one minds in Ireland. When you get there you are warmly welcomed by the Bourke family. The guests are a very cosmopolitan group; a great air of hospitality prevails and there is food galore of a very high standard.

Assolas Country House, Kanturk, Co. Cork.
Tel: 029-50015. Fax: 029-50795.

Reservations, USA: Robert Reid Associates. Toll Free 800-223-6510.
Proprietors: The Bourke family.
How to find
Take Mallow/Killarney road N.72 for 9 miles. Thence branch road to Kanturk
and sign-posted to Assolas.
Restaurant
Seating for 25.
Open 15 March to 1 November.
7.00 to 8.30 pm. IR£22.50. Service included.
Non-residents dinner booking essential.
Accommodation
Accommodation and breakfast from IR£35 inclusive low season; from IR£45
inclusive high season.
No. of bedrooms: 9.
All major credit cards accepted.
French spoken.

*Left: The original house, the centre of the present residence, seems
to date from the early 1600s. The shape of the windows with their
very old hand-blown glass with all its imperfections; the exterior
rough stone and mortar strengthened by the addition of horse hair
and ox blood; the walls, of great depth, four and a half foot thick,
are all in character. The eastern wing with beautifully rounded
frontage would appear to have been added a century later. The
large old flagstone kitchen on the ground floor was in everyday use
until 1915. Unfortunately no records are available to tell
us when the front wing was built.*

Flambéed Union Hall Prawns with Mushrooms

Per person:
5-6 large prawns
1 teaspoon butter
4 button mushrooms, thinly sliced
1-2 tablespoons brandy
4 fl oz (120 ml)/½ cup cream
chopped chives

Shell the prawns. Heat butter in a frying pan and sauté the prawns and mushrooms. Flambé with the brandy. Stir in the cream and chives. Allow to reduce until the cream has slightly thickened. Arrange the prawns on a warm plate and pour over the sauce.

Poached Fillet of Brill with a Fresh Basil Sauce

6 large brill fillets

Sauce
5 fl oz (150 ml)/¼ pint white wine
5 fl oz (150 ml)/¼ pint chicken stock
juice of ½ lemon
1 cup fresh basil, finely cut
1 shallot, finely chopped
4 oz (110 g)/½ cup unsalted butter
2 tablespoons cream ·
salt and pepper to taste

Reduce the wine with the shallots, until it becomes syrupy. Add the chicken stock with the lemon juice and reduce by half. Add the cream. Over a low heat gradually whisk in the butter. Add the basil and test for seasoning.
Preheat the oven to 400°F/200°C/Regulo 6.
Fillet and skin the brill. Season. Place the fish in an ovenproof dish. Pour over the wine and cover with tin foil. Place in oven for approx. 6 minutes.
To serve: pour sauce onto plate and lay the brill on top. Garnish with a little fennel.

Joe's Favourite Chocolate Cake

For the Cake

4 eggs
4 oz (110 g)/½ cup castor sugar
3 oz (85 g)/heaped ½ cup plain flour
1 oz (30 g) cocoa powder

Preheat oven 375°F/190°C/Regulo 5.

Whisk the eggs and sugar together until thick and mousse-like. Sieve the flour and cocoa together and gently fold into the egg mixture with a metal spoon. Carefully pour mixture into a 9 inch (15 cm) diameter cake tin. Bake for approx. 20-25 minutes. Turn out and cool on rack.

Stock syrup

8 oz (225 g)/1 cup granulated sugar
¼ pint (150 ml)/⅔ cup water
brandy to taste

Place sugar and water in a pan over low heat. Allow the sugar to dissolve slowly. Then bring to the boil and boil for 3 minutes. Allow to cool, then add brandy.

Chocolate filling and coating

   14 oz (400 g) chocolate (good quality plain)

   13 fl oz (400 ml)/1⅔ cups cream

Heat the cream in a saucepan until boiling. Remove from heat and beat in the chocolate pieces. Whisk until the mixture is completely homogenous.

For the filling

Beat half of the mixture (retaining the other half unbeaten for coating the cake) with an electric beater until mixture lightens in colour and stands in peaks. This takes quite a while.

To assemble

Split the cake into three layers. Brush each layer with the brandy syrup. Then sandwich the cake together with the filling. Pour the remaining unbeaten half of the coating/filling mixture over the top and sides of the cake. Allow to set.

If liked decorate the top and base of cake with piped rosettes of cream.

To get maximum 'Brownie points', serve with fresh strawberries and home-made vanilla ice cream.

Blairs Cove

BLAIRS COVE IS A GEORGIAN MANSION with adjoining cottages which have been converted into self-catering houses and flats. The main stable building in the 250-year-old stable yard has been stunningly converted into a stylish restaurant. Just to eat at Blairs makes a trip to Ireland worthwhile.

Blairs Cove Restaurant, Durrus, Nr Bantry, Co. Cork.
Tel: 027-61127.

Proprietors: Philippe and Sabine De Mey.
Open 1 March to 1 November, Tuesday to Saturday, 7.30 to 9.30 pm (also Mondays – July and August).

How to find
Blue gate one mile outside village of Durrus on Goleen/Barley Cove road.

Restaurant
Lunch 1.00-2.00 pm Sundays only.
Sunday lunch IR£12.00
Dinner IR£20.00.
German, Dutch and French spoken.

The house was built in 1720 and remodelled by Philippe and Sabine De Mey in 1981. The barn is now a double height structure of stripped stone dominated by a tiered fireplace based on a Swiss prototype to grill, smoke and mull, contrasting with thechandeliers and furniture from the De Mey family home in Bruges.

Smoked Salmon Mousse

8 fl oz (250 ml)/1 cup milk (boiled)
8 fl oz (250 ml)/1 cup cream
4 egg yolks
10½ oz (300 g) trimmings of smoked salmon (or ½ fresh salmon)
5 gelatine leaves
few slices salmon for mould

Oil mould and cover bottom with a thin layer of smoked salmon. Blend salmon in a food processor. Whisk egg yolks shortly in small saucepan and pour the boiled milk over. Stir with wooden spoon,add soaked gelatine leaves and allow this mixture to cool (e.g. in a cold water bath). As soon as the mixture starts setting, mix with smoked salmon, blend in whipped cream thoroughly and fill the mould. Let cool in fridge for a minimum of 2 hours, unmould onto a platter and serve immediately.

Escalopes of Veal Stuffed with Sweetbreads in a Mushroom Cream Sauce

3 escalopes
2 tablespoons butter
2 oz (55 g) mushroom slices

Farce
3 egg whites (chilled)
3½ fl oz (100 ml)/⅜ cup cream
pepper and salt
9 oz (250 g) sweetbreads, poached

Sauce
8 fl oz (250 ml)/1 cup homemade stock
8 fl oz (250 ml)/1 cup cream
salt and pepper

Put escalopes into a food processor and purée.

Farce

Beat the egg whites in a basin, add the cream and season with pepper and salt. Fold in sweetbreads which have been previously plucked apart. Season the escalope purée, divide into portions, flatten, place a tablespoon of farce on each and fold over. Fry them in butter. When nearly done, add mushroom slices. Remove meat and keep warm.

Sauce

Add the stock and cream and reduce until slightly thick. Check on the seasoning and serve.

Almond Roll

10 eggs

9 oz (250 g)/1⅛ cups sugar

9 oz (250 g)/1¾ cups flour

Beat sugar and eggs until pale; fold in flour gradually. Spread on a baking tray on greaseproof paper and bake at 400 °F/200 °C/Regulo 6 for 10 minutes. Take out of oven and place immediately between two dampened cloths.

Almond Filling

2 oz (55 g)/¼ cup sugar

1 dessertspoon water

3 egg yolks

4 leaves of gelatine

3½ oz (110 g)/½ cup Quark or cottage cheese

4 oz (110 g)/½ cup cream

1 dessertspoon sugar

a few drops of almond essence

Boil water and sugar for two minutes to make syrup. Allow to cool a little and then beat together with the egg yolks into a mousse. Add soaked gelatine and Quark or cottage cheese while the mixture is still warm. Whip the cream together with the dessertspoon of sugar and almond essence. Fold into the above mixture, then spread it out on the sponge and roll up.

Ballylickey Manor House

THE MANOR HOUSE IN THE PICTURESQUE VILLAGE of Ballylickey is in a formal park-like garden laid out along a river bank with sweeping vistas of Bantry Bay beyond, an area so beautiful that it has been praised in ballad, song and poetry for many centuries. A cluster of very attractive chalets and a grade A licensed restaurant surround a swimming pool in one part of the garden. The newly restored manor house contains more formal, ample and stylish suites most of which look out on the same photogenic view. The grounds were designed by George Graves' mother Kitty and contain a flooded rock garden. The house has mementoes of her brother-in-law, the poet, Robert Graves. The bright and sparkling interior decoration is the work of the present Mrs Graves.

Ballylickey Manor House, Bantry Bay, Co. Cork.
Tel: 027-50071. Fax: 027-50124.

Reservations: Robert Reid Associates, telephone: 800-223-6510.
Proprietors: Mr and Mrs George Graves.

How to find
On main road between Bantry and Glengariff.
Open end March to November.

Restaurant
À la carte lunch from 1.00-2.15 pm.
Dinner 7.30-9.00 pm from IR£19.50.
10% service charge.

Accommodation
Bed and breakfast from IR£35-IR£38.
Suites £90-IR£120.
No. of bedrooms: 6. *No. of suites:* 5
Visa and American Express cards accepted.
French spoken.

Built some 300 years ago, as a shooting lodge, by Lord Kenmare and extended by the Franco-Irish Graves family in 1950. Partially destroyed by a fire in 1984, it has now been restored to its original pre-1950 appearance.

Piccatas of Duck, Liver Foie Gras

21 oz (600 g) duck liver foie gras
30 stalks of green asparagus
water (to cook asparagus)
4-6 white mushrooms
1 lemon (juice only)
1 pint (600 ml)/2½ cups milk
4 fl oz (120 ml)/½ cup wine vinegar
4 fl oz (120 ml)/½ cup cream
salt and freshly ground black pepper
parsley to garnish

Clean and peel asparagus. Cut in half and cook heads and stalks separately, the stalks first as they take 4-6 minutes in boiling water with a pinch of salt, (heads, 2-4 minutes). Wash and slice mushrooms, sprinkle with lemon juice. Place the milk in a stainless steel saucepan, add mushrooms and cook gently for 10 minutes. Strain and place milk in a blender with the asparagus stalks and vinegar. Blend with cream to obtain a thick sauce. Season to taste. Cut foie gras in 12 slices. Cook without oil or grease in a non-stick pan for 1 minute on each side over a high flame until slightly golden. Remove and drain on absorbent kitchen paper. Spread sauce on serving dish. Place the foie gras slices on sauce and decorate with mushrooms, asparagus heads and parsley. Serve immediately.

Boiled Leg of Lamb with Caper Sauce

3 lb (1.35 kilo) leg of lamb
Bechamel sauce with capers and small pieces of butter

Weigh the lamb exactly and place in a pan just large enough to hold it. Cover the meat with a mild chicken or beef stock. The stock must be weak so as not to destroy the taste of the meat. If too strong, dilute with water. Remove the joint and heat stock to boiling. Return the meat to pan and simmer for a further 15 minutes per lb, not one minute more. Serve with a light Bechamel sauce to which capers have been added. Add enough butter (in small pieces) to suit your taste.

Irish Blackcurrant Cream

    11 oz (310 g) strawberries
    11 oz (310 g) wild strawberries
    11 oz (310 g) redcurrants
    11 oz (310 g) blackcurrants
    2 leaves gelatine
    17 fl oz (½ litre)/2 cups water
    9 o z (250 g)/1 cup castor sugar
    egg custard, whipped cream

Clean, top and tail the fruit. Cut strawberries into two or four
pieces depending on size. Divide strawberries and redcurrants
equally among 6 sundae glasses. Put gelatine to steep in small
quantity of cold water. Liquidise blackcurrants in blender. Heat the
water and sugar gently for 10 minutes. When boiling, add blackcurrants and gelatine. Pour mixture over strawberries and allow to set.
Make an egg custard. When cold, mix with whipped cream and
serve with the fruit.

The Park Hotel, Kenmare

THE PARK HOTEL, BUILT AS A HOTEL, has been successfully transformed into the elegance of a stately home. It has been filled with sumptuous works of art, Flemish tapestries and antiques. Notable is the 17th century Neapolitan water cistern painted with Venus arising out of the sea, hoisted on gilded dolphins. Nearby are the torch-bearing 'Peace and Plenty' (illustrated).

The hotel was opened as one of the Great Southern Railway Hotels in 1897 and sold in 1980. It was restored at enormous cost. Outside it still retains its solid castle-like Victorian facade, sitting in eleven acres of manicured garden. Inside the old railway hotel is now a place of baronial elegance. It has fifty bedrooms and six luxurious suites, all with marble bathrooms. The pride of the hotel is its food. Service, presentation and taste are quite exceptional, as is the setting. Added to all this you are in the middle of some of the loveliest countryside in Ireland.

The Park Hotel, Kenmare, Co. Kerry.
Tel: 064-41200. Fax: 064-41402.
Telex: 73905 PARK EI.

Reservations: Toll Free: 800-223-6472. N.Y. State: 800-522-5568. N.Y. City: 212-714-2323 or any Aer Lingus office.
Proprietor: Mr. Francis Brennan.
Open from Easter to New Year.

How to find
At top of town, beside Kenmare Golf Club.

Restaurant
Lunch from IR£16.50,13.00-14.00 hrs.
Dinner from IR£33.00,19.00-20.45 hrs.
Service charge optional.

Accommodation
Bed and breakfast from IR£64.00 to IR£90.00.
No. of bedrooms: 43.   *No. of suites:* 6.
Credit cards: M.C., Visa, Access, Diners.
French and German spoken.

The architect of The Park Hotel was James Franklin Fuller
who built Kylemore, Ashford Castle, Mt Falcon Castle
and Tinakilly House.

Avocado in Puff Pastry with a Fresh Tomato Sauce

1 large ripe avocado
2 oz (55 g) crabmeat
8 oz (225 g) puff pastry

Halve avocado, remove nut and skin. Sprinkle with lemon juice and season. Check crabmeat for shell. Squeeze out excessive liquid and season to taste. Fill half hollow with crabmeat. Roll pastry to 5 inches x 4 inches (12.5 x 10 cm), less than ⅛ inches (4 mm) thick. Place over each avocado half and fold under. Brush with egg and put on an oiled tray. Bake at 400 °F/200 °C/Regulo 6 for 5-7 minutes. Put sauce on plate, place avocado hollow side down and garnish.

Tomato Sauce

1 lb 3½ oz (550 g) ripe tomatoes, skinned and seeded
1½ oz (45 g) shallots/onions
½ clove garlic
2 sprigs thyme and rosemary
2 fl oz (60 ml)/¼ cup chicken stock (1 stock cube)
salt and freshly ground pepper

Make sure all the seeds, skin and excessive juice have been removed from the tomatoes. Sauté the shallots and garlic in a non-stick pan for 3-4 minutes, stirring constantly.
Add herbs and sauté for about one minute. Add tomatoes and stock. Simmer for 10-12 minutes. Remove herbs and purée the rest in a blender. Place sauce back in pan, bring to the boil and skim and season to taste.

Ribbons of Wild Duckbreast with Two Sauces

2 plump young birds
2 tablespoons oil
salt and pepper

Preheat oven to 350 °F/180 °C/Regulo 4. Prepare the ducks as fol-lows: Place in a roasting tray and sprinkle a little oil over them. Season with salt and freshly ground pepper. Roast until flesh is firm but still pink (approx. 1 hour). Allow to rest in a cool place for about 1 hour.

Remove the breasts from the two birds. Skin them and carve into six or eight thin slices depending on the size of the duckbreasts.

Juniper Berry Sauce

1 glass red wine

1 glass 'old port'

6 juniper berries

½ teaspoon thyme

½ pint (300 ml)/1¼ cups wild duck stock

a little cream (approx. 2 tablespoons) and unsalted butter

seasoning

Put the wine, port, juniper berries and thyme into a heavy saucepan and allow to reduce almost completely. Add the wild duck stock and allow to reduce further until the sauce is the required consistency. Strain through a sieve. Whisk in a little diced unsalted butter over a gentle heat. Season with salt and pepper. Add a couple of tablespoons of cream.

Pinekernel Sauce

2 oz (55 g) pinekernels

4 chopped shallots

hint of mace and coriander

squeeze of lemon juice

½ pint (300 ml)/1¼ cups cream

1 glass dry white wine

salt and pepper

Finely chop the pinekernels. Sweat the chopped shallots. Add the mace and coriander, a squeeze of lemon juice, then the cream, wine and pinekernels. Simmer gently for 4-5 minutes until the flavour from the pinekernels has been infused into the sauce. Strain, reheat and correct the seasoning.

Apple Pie du 'Parc'

Pastry

> 1 lb (450 g)/3½ cups flour
> 10 oz (285 g)/1¼ cups butter
> 4 oz (110 g)/½ cup sugar
> 2 eggs (whole)
> pinch salt

Rub together the flour, butter and salt. Add sugar and beaten eggs and bind together. Chill overnight.

Syrup

> ½ pint (300 ml)/1¼ cups water
> 4 oz (110 g)/½ cup sugar

Bring to the boil and add the juice of ½ lemon.

Filling

> 4-6 large cooking apples
> ½ pint (300 ml)/1¼ cups sugar syrup
> ½ tablespoon sultanas
> juice of ½ lemon
> ½ teaspoon cinnamon

Peel and slice apples thinly and place into hot syrup. Leave until syrup has cooled. Remove and mix in sultanas and cinnamon. Cool completely.

To assemble

Grease well a 10" (25 cm) flan ring and base. Roll out pastry to desired thickness and line mould. Trim edges. Place filling into pastry until just below level of rim. Roll out remaining pastry. Place on top. Seal edges by pressing between finger and thumb. Chill in refrigerator. Beat together 1 egg and 2 tablespoons of milk, and brush lightly onto pie. Bake at 380°F/190°C/Regulo 5-6 for ½-¾ hour or until golden brown. Serve hot or cold with lightly whipped cream or with hot fresh egg custard.

Doyle's Seafood Bar

THE DRIVE FROM KILLARNEY TO DINGLE is a tarmac roller-coaster that twists and turns along the shores of the Dingle Peninsula. The uncluttered beauty of the scenery improves with every bump and bend. At journey's end is Doyle's Seafood Bar, *the* place for excellent seafood.

John Doyle was a commercial offshore fisherman in Dingle when Stella started her seafood bar. With their combined expertise it thrived from early days. Stella has used the off-season break to study in some of the great kitchens in France and returned to upgrade and upmarket Doyle's. John eventually gave up fishing to concentrate on the restaurant. I spent two enthralling hours listening to the Doyles talking fish and fish cooking and saw their stainless steel, heat-controlled salt water tank in the 'out-back' where they store the daily catches of shellfish. John's knowledge of the fishermen and their fish ensures a great variety of the best fish – on your plate the day it is caught. The impressive wine list includes Californian, Australian and European vintages. As a sop to non-fish eaters the Doyles have a meat dish on their menu.

Doyle's Seafood Bar and Townhouse, John Street, Dingle, Co. Kerry.
Tel: 066-51174. Fax: 066-51816.

Reservations: Robert Reid Associates,telephone: 800-223-6510
Proprietors: John and Stella Doyle.
Open from mid-March to mid-November.
Restaurant closed all day Sunday.

How to find
In Dingle town centre.

Restaurant
Lunch from IR£5.00 approx. 12.30-2.15 pm.
Dinner from IR£15.00 approx. 6.00-9.00pm.
10% service charge.

Accommodation
Bed and breakfast: IR£25.00 double, IR£30.00 single.
No. of bedrooms: 8.
All major credit cards accepted.
French spoken.

A small village shop and pub built in 1790. It has its original
range and slate floor. Restored by Stella and John Doyle in 1968
and extended by them to accommodate the present restaurant. The
acquisition of the adjoining house by the Doyles has
extended their operation into an hotel.

Scallop Mousse with Beurre Blanc Sauce

6 oz (170 g) scallops

1 egg

4 fl oz (120 ml)/½ cup light cream

1 tablespoon softened butter

salt, pepper, nutmeg

Preheat oven to 425°F/220°C/Regulo 7. Put the scallops, a pinch of salt, ground pepper and nutmeg in a food processor. Mix thoroughly; add the egg. Allow mixer to turn once or twice, pour in the cream rapidly and then stop mixer. The ingredients should be cold. Butter the ramekin dishes and fill with the mousse. Place the ramekins in a dish of warm water and put into a pre-heated oven for 20 minutes.

Beurre Blanc Sauce

5 fl oz (150 ml)/¼ pint white wine

black peppercorns

sprig parsley

bay-leaf

1 tablespoon light cream

4 oz (110 g)/½ cup butter

In a heavy or copper saucepan put the wine, whole pepper, parsley and bay leaf. Reduce down to about 1 tablespoon of liquid. Add the cream. Let it boil to thicken slightly. Whisk in the butter in pieces. Season to taste.

Brown Trout with Mushroom Sauce

4 oz (110 g)/½ cup butter

3 oz (85 g)/approx ⅝ cup flour

6 trout

12 mushrooms

5 fl oz (150 ml)/⅝ cup fish stock

10 fl oz (300 ml)/1¼ cups sour cream

1 teaspoon lemon juice

1 teaspoon paprika

salt and pepper

Rinse the mushrooms. Place in a pan with the butter. Cook for about 10 minutes or until there is plenty of juice with the mush-

rooms. Add paprika and flour. Cook for a further few minutes. Add the stock, salt and pepper. Lastly add the sour cream and lemon juice. Bake the trout in a hot oven for about 12 minutes. Serve with the sauce.

Pear Cake

Ingredients for sponge base
3 oz (85 g)/6 tablespoons butter
3 oz (85 g)/⅓ cup sugar
1 egg
3 oz (85 g)/approx ⅝ cup self-raising flour

Ingredients for pear topping
16 oz (450 g) tin of pears, (drained)
7 leaves gelatine
13 oz (390 ml)/1½ cups whipped cream
2 egg whites, (whisked)
4 tablespoons Poire William liqueur

To make sponge
Put the first 4 ingredients into a food processor and beat. Put into an 8 inch (20 cm) lined and greased sponge tin. Cook at 350°F/180°C/Regulo 4, for 20 minutes. Leave to cool. Cut in half horizontally. Put into a loose bottomed 8 inch (20 cm) tin and pour pear mixture on top.

To make topping
Melt the gelatine in a little warm water. Add to puréed pears, with the Poire William, whipped cream and whisked egg whites. Pour over the sponge and leave to set.

MacCloskey's

TO GET INTO MACCLOSKEY'S you descend a staircase into a basement built into the side of a hill. A series of little vaulted cellar rooms offer views through tiny windows over the rooftops of Bunratty Folk Park and the battlements of the castle. Each little whitewashed dining-room accommodates 6-8 tables and one doesn't get the feeling of dining in an ordinary crowded restaurant. The meals are quite splendid with the most perfectly cooked and served vegetables. Halfway between Shannon airport and Limerick city, this very special restaurant has a marvellous address, Bunratty Castle for a neighbour and the Folk Park arrayed around it.

MacCloskey's Restaurant, Bunratty House Mews, Bunratty, Co. Clare.
Tel: 061-364082.

Proprietors: Gerry and Marie MacCloskey.
Open 7.00 pm to 10.00 pm, Tuesday to Saturday inclusive.
Closed 23 December to 23 January annually.

How to find
Take N18 from Limerick. Signposted at Bunratty.

Restaurant
Dinner table d'hôte IR£23.00 + 10% service charge.
American Express, Visa, Diner and Access credit cards accepted.

Bunratty House was built in 1804 by Thomas Studdert of
Bunratty Castle. It was intended as a temporary home until he
inherited the castle. However, as Bunratty House was more
comfortable than the nearby castle, Thomas Studdert stayed put
and the castle became a ruin. MacCloskey's Restaurant
is in the basement of this house.

Devilled Crab Cakes with Tarragon Sauce

6 oz (170 g)/¾ cup butter
½ green pepper, finely chopped
4 oz (110 g)/1 cup onion, finely chopped
½ pimento, chopped
1 teaspoon salt

½ teaspoon pepper
1 teaspoon thyme
1 tablespoon Worcestershire sauce
few drops Tabasco sauce
12 oz (340 g) white crabmeat
1 egg
flour, to dust cakes

Coating

2 eggs and 4 fl oz (120 ml)/½ cup milk beaten together

fine cracker crumbs, to roll cakes in

Melt butter in a saucepan over a low heat. In it sweat pepper, onion and pimento for approx. 25 minutes. Add salt, pepper, thyme, Worcestershire and Tabasco sauce. Cook for a further 10 minutes, stirring occasionally. Stir in crabmeat. Remove from heat and allow to cool. Whisk the egg and stir into the mixture.

Using a small round pastry cutter, cut into 1 inch (2.5 cm) cakes. Dust with flour and refrigerate for 15 minutes.

Dip the cakes into the egg and milk mixture, and roll in fine cracker crumbs. Preheat oven to 360 °F/180 °C/Regulo 4. Heat 1 inch (2.5 cm) of cooking oil in a deep pan to 360 °F/180-190 °C. Lower cakes in and deep fry for 1 minute on each side or until brown. Drain on absorbent paper. Bake in oven for 10-15 minutes. Serve immediately.

Tarragon Sauce

skin and bones of fish (e.g. salmon, sole, etc.)
12 tarragon leaves, chopped
5 fl oz (150 ml)/⅝ cup cream
3 oz (85 g)/6 tablespoons butter
1 teaspoon parsley, chopped
salt and pepper
lemon juice

Put skin and fish bones in a saucepan with 10 fl oz (300 ml)/1¼ cups of water. Cover and simmer for 25 minutes. Strain into another saucepan and boil hard until liquid is reduced to 2 tablespoons. Add tarragon and parsley, cover and cook for 1-2 minutes. Reserve this residue. Melt ½ oz (15 g)/1 tablespoon of butter. Add half the cream and the reserved liquid. Bring to the boil and add remaining cream. Whisk in the rest of the butter, piece by piece, over a gentle heat. Do not allow sauce to boil. Season with salt, pepper and lemon juice. Serve crab cakes on a warm plate in a pool of hot tarragon sauce.

Veal Steaks with Lemon

6-8 oz (170-225 g) veal per steak

Pare julienne strips of lemon peel from half a lemon. Put into a saucepan of cold water, bring to the boil and drain. Put in a saucepan with a soupspoon of water and a touch of sugar. Remove from heat when the water has evaporated and the julienne is a brilliant colour. Season the veal fillets and colour on both sides in a pan of heated butter. Remove the veal and set on a warm plate. Tip out the cooking butter, pour in 4 soupspoons of dry white wine and reduce by ⅔ over a low flame. Whisk in 1 oz (30 g)/2 tablespoons of butter to make an emulsion and add a teaspoon of chopped parsley. Season with salt and pepper. Pour the juices from the fillets into the sauce and coat the fillets. Garnish each fillet with a slice of lemon (without peel) and a pinch of the lemon julienne. Serve with a risotto or some vegetables cooked in butter.

Fresh Strawberry Soufflé

1¼ oz (35 g)/2½ tablespoons butter
3 tablespoons flour
2 tablespoons castor sugar
10 fl oz (300 ml)/1¼ cups cream (scalded)
5 eggs (separated)
6 oz (170 g) strawberries (chopped and hulled)

Melt the butter gently in a saucepan. Add the flour and cook for 2 minutes to make a blonde roux. Gradually add the scalded cream and cook over a low heat for 3-4 minutes. Whisk egg yolks and castor sugar until pale. Remove saucepan from heat and stir in egg mixture. Chop strawberries roughly, and fold into soufflé mixture. Butter 6 individual soufflé dishes and dust with castor sugar. Whisk egg whites until stiff and lightly fold into mixture. Turn into prepared dishes and cook in a pre-heated oven at 450°F/250°C/Regulo 9 for 10 minutes or until puffed and brown on top. Decorate with sifted icing sugar and slices of strawberries. Serve immediately.

Gregans Castle Hotel

GREGANS CASTLE HOTEL IS A GOOD CENTRE for touring the Burren. The Burren occupies about 100 square miles of Co. Clare. Geologists call it 'karst' after similar regions in Yugoslavia. The area is of outstanding interest to geologists and botanists. The entire region has a complex system of underground lakes and turloughs (lakes which disappear overnight) and streams which disappear into pot holes. There is much evidence of prehistoric occupation with numerous dolmens and forts. Visually it resembles a lunar-like landscape with its own distinctive flora.

Gregans Castle Hotel, Ballyvaughan, Co. Clare. (via Galway).
Tel: +353.65.77005. Fax: +353.65.77111.

Reservations: Call us direct within Ireland 065-77005; from USA 011.353.65.77005; from UK 010.353.65.77005 or within USA 800.223.6510. Robert Reid Associates.
Proprietors: Peter and Moira Haden.
Open 7 April to 31 October.

How to find
On Route N67 between Ballyvaughan and Lisdoonvarna. One hour's drive from Shannon Airport.

Restaurant
Dinner IR£20.00 from 7.00 to 8.30 pm. 12½% service charge.

Accommodation
Bed and breakfast from IR£33.00
No. of bedrooms: 10. *No. of suites:* 6.
Credit Card: Visa.
English and French spoken.

The original Tower House belonged to the O'Loughlins, Princes of Burren who intermarried with the Protestant Martyns of Galway in 1632 and so preserved their Estates. The 18th century house was extended in 1880, restored and made into an hotel in 1965. The original stove and arched fireplace of the kitchen survive in the lounge with the chair of Edward Martyn recently acquired by the present owners.

Home Smoked Sausages

12 of your favourite pork sausages
2 bacon rashers
garlic
green salad
oil (preferably olive)
vinegar
seasoning

Pierce each sausage in about four places and insert a sliver of garlic and a tiny piece of bacon rasher. Using one of those simple fisherman's smokers, (available in most sports goods shops), smoke the sausages for about half an hour. Leave to cool in the smoker. When cool, cut each sausage into small pieces about ½ inch (1.5 cm) long. Make a green salad of available items such as lettuce, green peppers, thin cucumber slices, and endives. Make a salad dressing using two parts oil to one part vinegar. Add seasoning to taste, and toss together the salad, sausage pieces and dressing. Serve slightly chilled.

Brochette of Fruit and Chicken with Avocado Sauce

6 chicken breasts, skinned and boned
juice of one large lemon
juice of one orange
6 tablespoons white wine (dry)
1 teaspoon basil
1 teaspoon thyme
ground black pepper
2 green or red peppers cut into chunks
3 small onions cut into quarters
12 prunes (soaked overnight)
2 firm bananas
12 rashers streaky bacon

Avocado Sauce
  2 ripe avocados
  juice of 1 lemon
  8 fl oz (250 ml)/1 cup natural yoghurt
  chopped chives
  chopped parsley
  seasoning

In a bowl, place the lemon juice, white wine, seasoning and herbs. Into this marinade place the chicken breasts (cut up into good size cubes), and leave for 1-2 hours. Meanwhile, cut the peppers into chunks, the onions into quarters, and the bananas into strips about 2 inches (5 cm) long. Remove the stones from the prunes. Stretch each rasher using the back of a knife and make sure the rind has been removed. Wrap a piece of the stretched rasher around each prune and each slice of banana. With an eye to appearance, carefully arrange all these ingredients, including the chicken, onto 6 skewers. Brush with the marinade juices and grill most carefully for about 15 minutes until you are satisfied that the chicken is cooked through. Do not over-brown or burn. Meanwhile make the sauce. Mix together the flesh of the ripe avocados and other ingredients. An electric blender is best for this, although it can be done by hand with a fork. With the sauce in a jug, warm gently by placing jug into a saucepan of hot water and stirring. Spread the sauce thinly yet consistently over a warm plate, and place the brochette of fruit and chicken in the centre. Carefully withdraw the skewer before serving.

Oranges in Grand Marnier

  7 large oranges (with as few pips as possible)
  6 oz (170 g)/¾ cup castor sugar
  6 tablespoons Grand Marnier liqueur

Peel the zest off one orange and cut into very thin slices. Squeeze the juice from this orange and reserve. Cut all the pith and peel from remaining six oranges, and cut into thin slices. Arrange these slices, overlapping, in a bowl. Mix together the orange juice and Grand Marnier and pour over the oranges. Sprinkle over all the sugar. Chill well (preferably overnight). Just before serving, sprinkle with thin slices of zest.

Drimcong House Restaurant

IN THE GALWAY AREA, YOU COULDN'T DO BETTER than seek out Drimcong House. With a skilled menu, expertly executed, it is one of those wonderful and unique places that one could hardly fault. In the kitchen Gerry Galvin presents his platters like rare works of art, and even if you sit down with the best 'must watch my weight' attitude, I defy you to keep it up beyond the first ounce (28 g!) of the first course.

Drimcong House Restaurant, Moycullen, Co.Galway.
Tel: 091-85115/85585.

Proprietors: Gerard and Marie Galvin.
Chef: Gerard Galvin.
Closed January and February.
Children welcome.

How to find

Drimcong lies one mile west of Moycullen on the main Galway/Clifden road.

Restaurant

Open for dinner Tuesday to Saturday inclusive.
Private lunch parties by arrangement.
Dinner à la carte, 5 course table d'hôte dinner IR£15.95 and a vegetarian menu IR£13.95.
Children's 3 course dinner at IR£7.50.
10% service charge.
Major credit cards accepted.
Irish, English, French, German and Spanish spoken.

Original 17th century lakeside house just outside Galway,
remodelled in 18th century. It has exceptionally fine carved stone
Queen Anne doorcase. Owned and run as a restaurant
by Gerry and Marie Galvin.

Mussels in a Lettuce Sauce

1 dozen plump mussels per person
1 cup of 'lambs' lettuce
2 oz (55 g)/4 tablespoons unsalted butter
½ pint (300 ml)/1¼ cups cream
¼ pint (150 ml)/⅝ cup mussel liquor
white pepper

Steam and shell mussels and keep warm. Combine lettuce and butter in a food processor until amalgamated. Keep chilled. Reduce cream and mussel liquor over high heat for 3 minutes. Reduce heat, add butter and whisk until incorporated in the cream. Add mussels and serve with a pinch or two of white pepper.

N.B. Salt should not be used at any stage in this recipe.

Roast Pheasant and Game 'Jus'

6 oven-ready pheasants with legs removed
a little egg white
a little whipped cream
1 tablespoon finely chopped shallot
¼ pint (150 ml)/⅝ cup red wine
1 tablespoon sherry vinegar
1 pint (600 ml)/2¼ cups game stock
hazelnut oil
seasoning

Preheat the oven to 400°F/200°C/Regulo 6.
Blend the leg meat in a food processor, and fold in enough beaten egg white and cream to make a mousse. Put in 'timbale' moulds and chill. Over high heat cook shallot, wine and vinegar until syrupy. Add stock and reduce briskly for ten minutes, at which time the *jus* should be gamey and flavoursome. Season if necessary. In a hot oven, roast seasoned pheasants in hazelnut oil for 20 minutes, turning once. At the same time bake the timbales for the same duration, in a bain-marie. Unmould the timbales, remove and carve breasts, and serve together with hot *jus*.

Avocado Sorbet

3 medium avocados
juice of 1 lemon
1 tablespoon honey
1 tablespoon vodka
salt and white pepper
1 egg white

Peel and chop avocado and toss in a mixture of lemon juice, honey, vodka, salt and pepper. Liquidise. Incorporate beaten egg white and process in an ice-cream machine or sorbetiére. Store in freezer and allow to soften a little before use. Decorate with herbs or flowers such as borage or lemon balm.

Currarevagh House

A TRIP TO IRELAND WOULD BE INCOMPLETE without taking in Connemara in the west. It is a sparsely populated, picturesque landscape of mountains, forests and lakes extending to the Atlantic coast.

In the heart of all this is Currarevagh House, serenely situated by Lough Corrib on a 150-acre woodland demesne. One might say this is what country-house living is all about – intimate, friendly and comfortable, with everything just right. If one can bear to leave such idyllic surroundings, there is the Yeats Country to explore further north, or the Burren and Galway to the south. For the fisherman, there is the added attraction of the well-stocked lake.

The convivial tea time in the lounge is a treat worth hurrying back for. The bedrooms are large, fresh and comfortable. The dinners are great and so too are the diners.

Currarevagh House, Oughterard, Connemara, Co. Galway.
Tel: 091-82312/82313.

Proprietors: Harry and June Hodgson.
Open from spring to October.

How to find
Take the N59 (Galway-Clifden) to Oughterard. Turn right in village square and follow the 'Lakeshore' road for 4 miles (6 km).

Restaurant
Dinner IR£15.25 at 8.00 pm.
10% service charge.

Accommodation
Bed and breakfast from IR£33.00.
3-6 day (half board) rate IR£45.00 per person per day. Weekly (half board) rate IR£285.00 per person. Out-of-season house parties of 8 or more welcome (excluding Christmas).
No. of bedrooms: 15.
No credit cards.
French spoken.

The house was built by the Hodgson family, ancestors of the present occupants. Built in 1847, it replaced an earlier dwelling. Conceived on a grand scale in the Italian manner, it has the air of a London club magically wafted onto a wooded promontory, to overlook the forests and islands of Lough Corrib. The windows are early examples of plate glass; the fireplaces are robustly Victorian.

Terrine of Smoked Salmon

6 small slices of smoked salmon
8 oz (225 g) flaked smoked salmon
2 level dessertspoons of powdered gelatine mixed with ½ pint
(300 ml)/1¼ cups warm water
2 egg yolks
1 heaped teaspoon Dijon mustard
1 heaped teaspoon tomato purée
juice of 2 lemons
6 fl oz (170 ml)/¾ cup nut oil
8 fl oz (250 ml)/1 cup milk
2 oz (55 g)/¼ cup cream
plenty of salt and black pepper

Dissolve the gelatine in the water over a gentle heat and leave to cool. Dip slices of smoked salmon into the gelatine and line the bottom of six ramekin dishes. Put yolks, lemon juice, mustard, tomato purée, oil, salt and pepper into a liquidiser and combine. Put this mixture into a jug and add the gelatine. Put flaked smoked salmon, milk and cream into the liquidiser and combine. Add this mixture to the above and pour into ramekin dishes. Leave to set for 4-6 hours and turn out.
Serve with herbs.

Baked Stuffed Leg of Veal with Lemon Sauce

6 lb (2.7 kg) boned leg of veal
2 oz (55 g)/¼ cup margarine
1 onion
4 oz (110 g)/1 cup breadcrumbs
thyme and sage
grated peel of 1 lemon
salt and pepper

Remove as much fat as is possible from the veal and leave flat. Combine all the other ingredients and make the stuffing. Spread over the veal and roll; secure with string. Put the veal into a large baking dish in which there is one inch of water. Spread a liberal amount of margarine over the veal and cover with foil. Bake in a hot oven for 20 minutes and then reduce to 350°F/180°C/Regulo 4 for ¾ hour. Remove foil, brown in a hot oven for 10 minutes and slice it when hot.

Lemon Sauce

 2 oz (55 g)/¼ cup margarine
 1 onion, diced
 2 oz (55 g)/scant ½ cup flour
 ½ pint (300 ml)/1¼ cups chicken stock
 2 egg yolks
 3 oz (85 g)/⅜ cup cream
 salt and pepper
 juice of 2 lemons

Melt margarine, add the diced onion and cook until soft. Add flour and make a roux. Gradually add the chicken stock and cook for five minutes. Strain and leave to cool. Make a liaison with the yolks and cream and add to the above mixture. Add the lemon juice, season to taste and serve hot with the veal.

Chocolate Praline Pudding

3 oz (85 g) plain chocolate
1 pkt of sponge fingers
1 tablespoon Tia Maria
1 tablespoon brandy
1 tablespoon cold strong coffee
1 tablespoon milk
¾ pint (450 ml)/1¾ cups cream
1 tablespoon castor sugar
6 oz (170 g)/1½ cups coarse praline

Melt the chocolate and leave to cool. Mix the Tia Maria, brandy, coffee and milk. Dip half the sponge fingers into it and line the bottom of a long tin with them. Whip the cream and add the castor sugar and cooled chocolate. Spread half over the biscuits, add half the praline then the rest of the biscuits dipped in the coffee solution. Put most of the remaining praline on top of the biscuits. If there is any of the coffee solution left over, combine it with the remaining cream and spread over the praline. Leave in the freezer for 2-3 hours. Turn out and sprinkle with praline.

Cashel House

A FEATURE OF CASHEL HOUSE is the award-winning 50-acre garden, with rhododendrons, azaleas, camellias and beautiful rare magnolias. Situated at the head of Cashel Bay with its own little beach, the house has the Atlantic Ocean almost on its doorstep. Inside it is warm and comfortable with turf fires and fresh flowers everywhere. The bedrooms are excellent, attractively furnished with character and charm. I found the food and wine very good. A word of warning – there are two Cashels on the map of Ireland – don't turn up at the other one and ask for the Atlantic Ocean!

Cashel House Hotel, Cashel, Co. Galway.
Tel: 095-31001. Fax: 095-31077.
Telex: 50812.

Reservations: USA Toll Free 800-223-6764 nationwide. Robert Reid Assoiates: 800-223-6510 (Toll Free).
Proprietors: Dermot and Kay McEvilly.
Open 15 February to 15 November.
How to find
On main Galway/Clifden road N59, turn left at Recess.
Restaurant
Dinner IR£21.50 from 7.30 to 8.30 pm
12½% service charge.
Accommodation
Bed and breakfast from IR£41.50.
No. of bedrooms: 17.   *No. of suites:* 13.
All major credit cards accepted.
Irish, French and German spoken.

Cashel House, built in 1850 for Captain Hazel by Geoffrey
Emmerson who is said to have designed it. Kay McEvilly, his
great-grand-daughter, and her husband Dermot
are the present owners.

Seafood Pâté

4 oz (110 g) smoked salmon
4 oz (110 g) smoked mackerel, skinned
5 oz (140 g) seafood (scallops, lobster pieces etc.)
12-16 oz (340-450 g)/1½-2 cups soft butter
salt and pepper
chopped chives
lemon juice
spinach leaves (cooked)

First layer
Blend smoked salmon and lemon juice. Add the butter (7 oz /200 g/⅞ cup) in small bits very carefully so that the butter does not curdle.

Second layer
Blend smoked mackerel and lemon juice. Add the butter (4 oz/ 110 g/½ cup) in small bits. Blend carefully until of smooth consistency.

Third layer
Blend scallops, lobster, and lemon juice. Add the butter. (5 oz /140 g/⅝ cup) and salt, pepper and chives. Line a pâté dish with grease-proof paper. Separate each pâté with spinach leaves and chill.

Chicken with Orange and Mustard Sauce

3.5 lb (1.6 kg) chicken, jointed
4 fl oz (120 ml)/½ cup orange juice
½ tablespoon butter
½ tablespoon oil
8 fl oz (250 ml)/1 cup water
1 tablespoon Dijon mustard
1 tablespoon brown sugar
1 pint (600 ml)/2½ cups cream
salt and pepper

Marinate the chicken overnight in the orange juice and water.
Remove from the marinade and sauté the chicken pieces in oil and
butter until brown. Set chicken aside and keep warm.
To make the sauce: add the marinade, Dijon mustard, brown sugar
and cream to the pan and reduce by a third. Add the chicken pieces
and simmer gently for 10 minutes or until the chicken is cooked.
Season and serve.

Yoghurt Mousse, with Pineapple, Strawberries or Kiwi Fruit and a Caramel Sauce

2½ fl oz (75 ml) milk
4 egg yolks
1 oz (30 g)/2 tablespoons sugar
6 leaves gelatine
¾ pint (450 ml)/1⅞ cups yoghurt
juice of 1 lemon
½ pint (300 ml)/1¼ cups cream
4 egg whites

Sauce
7 oz (200 g)/⅞ cup sugar
juice and zest of 2 oranges
juice of 1 lemon
3 oz (85 g)/⅜ cup apricot purée

2-3 fl oz/(60-85 ml) Crème de Cacao or Curaçao

1 fresh or tinned pineapple

or 8 oz (225 g) fresh or frozen strawberries

or 2 kiwi fruits sliced

To prepare the mousse, bring the milk to the boil. Cream the egg yolks and sugar well; gradually add the boiled milk and mix well. Return to the heat, stirring constantly until the mixture starts to thicken, but do not boil. Soak the gelatine in a little cold water, then stir into the hot mixture. Add the yoghurt and lemon juice. Whisk until smooth. Leave to cool. Whip the egg whites and fold in the sugar. When the yoghurt mixture is cold fold in the cream (whipped) and egg whites. Pour the mixture into individual dishes and place in the fridge to set.

To make the sauce: melt the sugar over heat until it becomes a slightly dark caramel. Add the juice and zest of the oranges, lemon and apricot purée. Mix well and add the Crème de Cacao and recook the sauce slightly. Wash and cut fruit and arrange on the set mousse. Coat with the sauce, just before serving.

Rosleague Manor

IF YOU ENJOY BEING A GUEST in a period house, you couldn't do better than stay at Rosleague, a Regency manor house commanding a superb position on the Atlantic coast of Connemara. Furnished with well-chosen antiques, it has been turned into a place of infinite charm by brother and sister team Anne and Paddy Foyle. Guests have included many of the world's rich and famous. The food has won prestigious awards internationally and the Irish Tourist Board's award of excellence.

Rosleague Manor Hotel, Letterfrack, Co. Galway.
Tel: 095-41101. Fax: 095-41168

Reservations: by telephone, fax or post. For reservations U.S.A.
call Robert Reid Associates, 800-223-6510.
Proprietors: Anne and Patrick Foyle.
Open from Easter to early November.

How to find
Off main Galway to Clifden road turn right at Recess,
or go to Clifden and turn right to Letterfrack.

Restaurant
Dinner IR£19.50 from 8.00-9.30 pm.
No service charge.

Accommodation
Bed and breakfast from IR£30 to IR£45.
No. of bedrooms: 15.   *No. of suites:* 4.
Most credit cards accepted.
French, German and Spanish spoken.

A regency villa of the 1820s. The gardens were extended by
Edward and Liz O'Brien who bought it in 1950 from the Land
Commission and sold it to Paddy and Anne Foyle in 1971. A
wing was added by architect Leo Mansfield. The house has
spectacular views of Ballinakill Bay, the
Twelve Pins and Kylemore.

Mulligatawny Soup

Rosleague's most requested recipe

   1 small onion, diced
   1 tablespoon vegetable oil
   1 heaped tablespoon hot curry powder
   1 heaped tablespoon tomato purée
   ½ cup uncooked rice
   2½ pints (1.4litres)/6¼ cups good chicken stock
   1 small cooking apple, cored and diced
   at least 1 tablespoon lime juice cordial.

Garnish: cream, paprika

Fry the onion in a little oil until soft, *not* brown; stir in the curry powder, tomato purée and rice. Stir quickly together but do not let it burn. Pour on the chicken stock and let the whole lot come to the boil. Add the diced apple and when the rice is completely soft put the mixture through a blender or mouli.

The soup must be really smooth and 'silky' in texture. Return to the pan and add the lime juice cordial to taste or, if you prefer, a little pineapple juice. At this stage a little cream wouldn't go astray.

Heat gently again but do not boil. If the mixture gets too thick, thin it down with a little chicken stock.

Garnish with a swirl of cream and a sprinkling of paprika.

Stuffed Turkey Breton-Style

Stuffing
some white or brown stale breadcrumbs (approx. 3 cups)
1 lb (450 g) pork sausages
5 oz (150 g)/1 cup raisins
20 soaked and stoned prunes
2½ oz (70 g)/½ cup chopped or flaked almonds (optional but nice!)
large glass of port (or cooking sherry can be substituted)
all the giblets especially the liver finely chopped – omit the neck of course!
some thyme, lovage and any other desired herbs
2 chopped onions and a little garlic

Fry the onions and garlic in lots of butter until soft, *not* brown. Add other ingredients and, depending on consistency, add or omit more breadcrumbs. The mixture should hold its shape but not be too dry – use your judgement. Stuff and roast turkey in the normal way.

Simple Almond and Walnut Cake (top-secret recipe)

10 oz (280 g)/2 cups white flour
8 oz (225 g)/1 cup castor sugar
2-3 level teaspoons baking powder
6 fl oz (175 ml)/¾ cup milk
4 oz (110 g)/½ cup softened butter and vegetable shortening mixed
2 eggs
1 teaspoon almond essence
2 oz (55 g)/½ cup finely chopped walnuts (or 1 small packet)

Measure everything except nuts into a large mixing bowl. Blend at low speed until mixed (about 3 minutes) then at high speed. Finally fold in the chopped nuts and pour into two loaf tins. Bake for 50-60 minutes 350°F/180°C/Regulo 4-5.

Newport House

A STATELY IVY-COVERED MANSION rich in history and hand-somely decorated with period furniture. It has elegance and atmosphere. Bedrooms are of country house size. The food comes mainly from the garden and farm, the fish from the private fishery and the salmon is home smoked. The splendid meal I remember with pleasure. If fishing is your 'thing', it would be hard to find a more idyllic place.

Newport House, Newport, Co. Mayo.
Tel: 098-41222.
Fax: 098-41613. Telex 53740.

Reservations: by post, telephone, fax or telex. In USA Robert Reid Associates, 800-223-6510 (Toll Free) or direct.
Proprietors: Kieran and Thelma Thompson.
Open 19 March to 30 September.

How to find
On Westport to Newport road.

Restaurant
Dinner, IR£23.00 from 7.30 pm to 9.30 pm.
Prices inclusive of VAT and service charge.

Accommodation
Bed and breakfast IR£40.00.
No. of bedrooms: 20.
All major credit cards accepted.
French spoken.

Newport House was once the seat of the O'Donnells, one of the 'Wild Geese' families, Counts of the Holy Roman Empire. It is sited overlooking the Newport River. Its origin is the mid-18th century. The entrance hall leads into a small domed lobby that very dramatically opens up to a Regency arched and galleried staircase hall lit by a central lantern and elliptical dome. Recent restoration and decoration was completed in 1987 by owners Mr and Mrs Kieran Thompson.

Fresh Prawns En-croûte with Provençale Sauce

8 oz (225 g) puff pastry
1 lb (450 g) fresh prawn tails, unpeeled
2 oz (55 g)/¼ cup garlic butter
1 egg

Roll out puff pastry in a rectangular shape ⅛ inch (3 mm) thick. Set aside for 20 minutes. Cut out four 1.5 inch (4 cm) square pieces. Place fresh *unpeeled* prawns of equal quantity on the centre of each square. Put ½ oz (15 g)/1 tablespoon of garlic butter on top of prawns. Brush the four corners with beaten up egg. Fold opposite four corners to meet in centre and brush with the remainder of egg. Gently place the pastry case on a floured baking sheet and leave in a cool place for approx. one hour.

Provençale Sauce

2 oz (55 g)/4 tablespoons garlic butter
1 small onion, finely chopped
pinch of fresh thyme
1 lb (450 g) tomatoes (5 large)

Melt the garlic butter, add the finely chopped onion and thyme. Cook gently without colouring the butter. Blanch and dice tomatoes, then add to the mixture. Cook slowly for 10 minutes. Season with salt and pepper.

To serve

Cook the pastry cases in a hot oven 400 °F/200 °C/Regulo 6 for about 15 minutes. When cooked, place a generous spoonful of Provençale sauce on the plate. Place the pastry case in the middle.

Parslied Chicken Guerard

1 chicken 3.5 lb (1.575 kilos)

Stuffing 1

¾ oz (20 g)/1½ tablespoons butter

1 tablespoon parsley

1 tablespoon water

1 teaspoon salt

½ teaspoon pepper

2 oz (55 g)/¼ cup natural yoghurt

juice of 1 lemon

Stuffing 2

3 tablespoons parsley (chopped)

1 tablespoon chives

1 teaspoon tarragon

2 tablespoons shallots

2 oz (55 g)/½ cup mushrooms

2 oz (55 g)/2 rashers streaky bacon

Sauce

¾ oz (20 g)/1½ tablespoons butter

1 lb (450 g) chopped shallots

1 tablespoon sherry vinegar

6½ fl oz (200 ml)/¾ cup stock

4 tablespoons cream

1 oz (30 g)/2 tablespoons softened butter

¾ oz (20 g)/1½ tablespoons tomato pulp (no skin)

1 tablespoon chervil

Blend together all ingredients in stuffing 1. Put the mixture into a large bowl. Mix in the stuffing 2 ingredients and beat together with a fork to obtain a smooth stuffing.

Stuffing the chicken

Lift the skin away from the breast and legs of the chicken (by sliding your fingers between the skin and flesh) working carefully and slowly to avoid tearing the skin. Insert the stuffing between the flesh and skin, patting it with your fingers in an even layer over the breast and thighs.

Cooking the chicken

Season the inside of the chicken with salt and pepper and roast (breast upwards) for 45 minutes (450°F/230°C/Regulo 8) basting frequently. When the chicken is cooked, remove from oven. Transfer to dish and keep hot.

Preparing the sauce

Remove fat from the roasting tin, replace it with ⅓ oz (10 g/¾ tablespoon) butter and add finely chopped shallots. Cook without colouring, add the sherry vinegar, scraping up all the caramelised roasting juices. Reduce by ¾. Add chicken stock and cream. Reduce by ⅓. Finally beat in 1 oz (30 g)/2 tablespoons of butter in pieces. Strain the sauce through a wire sieve, add diced tomatoes and chervil. Keep hot in bain-marie.

Serving the chicken

Cut the chicken into 6 pieces, leaving one piece of breast and thigh together. Arrange the pieces of chicken on serving dish and coat with hot sauce. Serve with buttered broccoli and boiled new potatoes.

Crème Brûlée

½ pint (300 ml)/1¼ cups cream
½ pint (300 ml)/1¼ cups milk
3 eggs
2 tablespoons vanilla castor sugar (or unflavoured sugar and 1
teaspoon vanilla essence)
brown sugar

Empty cream and milk into a thick-bottomed saucepan, bringing
the creamy milk not quite to the boil. Lightly whisk the eggs with
the sugar and vanilla. Add to the warmed creamy milk mixture.
Make sure the cream mixture is not too hot (otherwise it will
curdle). Half-fill a roasting pan with boiling water to make a bain-
marie and ladle the cream and egg mixture into small earthenware
custard dishes. Stand the puddings in the pan and cook for 2-2½
hours at 250°F/130°C/Regulo ½.
These puddings require gentle cooking; otherwise they will curdle.
Test to see whether they have set by shaking gently. Cool overnight. The puddings must be cold before the brûlée is added.
An hour before you serve the crème brûlée, sprinkle brown sugar
over each one and place under the grill until the sugar melts,
spreads and browns. Watch over them to see the sugar does not
burn.
Serve with *Langue du Chat* finger biscuits.

Enniscoe House

THE NAME 'INNISCOE' MEANS 'Island of the Hound' and it is said to have originated from a family far back in Irish history, who were in possession of these lands and who were renowned breeders of greyhounds. The history of the house and estate revolves around the families and ancestors of the present occupants and is meticulously documented through family records of birth, marriages and deaths from 1163 to the present day.

Enniscoe is now a country house hotel with a comfortable aura – and with windows overlooking the peaceful parklands and distant lake, antique furniture and family portraits everywhere. My bedroom was of noble size complete with four poster bed. The home smoked trout with yoghurt sauce I had for dinner was excellent. If you plan to see Ireland, this is it – amid green fields and mountains. Even when it rains (and it does) it never pours – it's just soft Irish rain which keeps the 'Emerald' in the landscape.

Enniscoe House, Castlehill, Nr Crossmolina, Ballina, Co. Mayo. Tel: 096-31112. Telex: c/o 40855

Reservations: USA Robert Reid Associates or call direct.
Proprietor: Susan Kellett.
Open 1 April to 14 October and 31 December to 1 February.

How to find
Enniscoe is two miles south of Crossmolina on the road to Pontoon and Castlebar. It is 12 miles from Ballina.

Restaurant
Dinner IR£16.00 from 8.00 to 9.00 pm.
No service charge for residents.

Accommodation
Bed and breakfast from IR£30.00. Family rates on request.
No. of bedrooms: 6.
AMEX, visa, Access cards accepted.

*Enniscoe House is an early 18th century, West of Ireland,
four-storied manor house, its architecture attributed to John
Roberts. Extended in 1790 and disguised to make a square double-
storied house on a grander scale. The new rooms encase the
surprise of an elliptical staircase curving dizzily upwards beneath
a glazed dome. Paintings are by the surrealist artist Mrs
Nicholson who is mother of the owner.*

Broccoli Soup with Garlic Croûtons

2 medium onions
2 oz (55 g)/4 tablespoons butter
2 lbs (900 g) broccoli
2 pints (1.14 litres)/5 cups chicken stock
salt and pepper
2 slices stale white bread
clove garlic, crushed
1 oz (30 g)/2 tablespoons butter

Peel and chop onions. Soften in butter over a gentle heat. Add broccoli, turn over in the butter and onion. Add stock and seasoning. Cook gently for about 15 minutes. Put through sieve or purée in food processor. Thin if necessary with a little milk; check seasoning. Fry bread cubes in garlic and butter until golden brown. Serve soup very hot with the fried croûtons.

Hot Smoked Trout with Yoghurt and Herb Sauce

1 trout per person, cleaned and filleted
4 oz (110 g)/½ cup natural yoghurt
fresh herbs
lemon juice
salt and pepper
cornflour, 1 teaspoon

Use sea trout if possible. Rainbow trout will also be quite successful. If you have a home smoker, use warm from smoker. If not, wrap trout in foil, with butter and seasoning and cook in a hot oven for 10 minutes.

Sauce

Put yoghurt into a heavy saucepan. Stabilise by adding a teaspoon of cornflour. Bring slowly to boil, stirring in one direction only. Take off heat at once, add generous amount of chopped herbs (parsley, lemon balm, fennel), lemon juice, salt and pepper.

Cinnamon Apple Flan

8 oz (225 g)/1⅔ cups plain flour
pinch salt
6 oz (170 g)/¾ cup butter
2 egg yolks
2 oz (55 g)/¼ cup castor sugar
2 teaspoons cinnamon
3-4 firm eating apples
Bailey's cream liqueur
brown sugar

To make the sugar crust pastry, sift in the cinnamon with the flour and castor sugar. Rub in the butter till it resembles fine bread-crumbs. Combine with the egg yolks. Mix to a dough. Leave to rest. Peel and slice apples neatly. Put in heavy saucepan with 2-3 table-spoons liqueur. Cook very gently for 5 minutes. Roll out pastry, line an 8 inch (20 cm) flan tin with removable bottom. Place apples and liqueur in pastry case; add a little more liqueur if too dry. Sprinkle generously with brown sugar. Cook in a hot oven until pastry case is done and the sugar is caramelised. Serve with whipped cream.

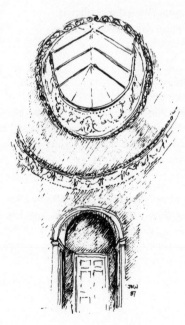

Mount Falcon Castle

MOUNT FALCON IS ABOVE ALL A HOTEL WITH PERSONALITY – that of the owner, Constance Aldridge, who has managed it for over 50 years. Most of the guests are fisherfolk and shooters who return year after year. They fish all day and exchange fishy tales in the evening in the convivial atmosphere of the bar or library. If you are not a dedicated golfer or fisherperson you can sit in the beautiful garden, go sightseeing in Co. Mayo, or explore the pubs and shops in Ballina. The evening meal, served on the long mahogany table under the chandeliers is a truly baronial affair. Fish and game rank high on the menu and the milk, eggs and vegetables come from the castle farm. The bar is well stocked and run on a 'help yourself and sign the book' arrangement.

Mount Falcon Castle, Ballina, Co. Mayo.
Tel: 096-21172. Telex: 40899. Fax: 21172

Reservations: Robert Reid Associates.
Proprietor: Mrs C. Aldridge.
Open Easter to January 31. Closed Christmas week.

How to find
On main Ballina/Foxford road.

Restaurant
Lunch on request, residents only.
Dinner IR£17.00 at 8.00 pm.
10% service charge.

Accommodation
Bed and breakfast with bath from IR£30-IR£37.50 per person.
Demi-pension from IR£42.50-IR£50 per person.
50% reduction for children under 10 years sharing parents' bedroom. Under 3 years free.
No. of bedrooms: 10.
All major credit cards accepted.
French spoken.

The castle is a grey stone, turreted mansion built in 1876 by architect John Franklin Fuller. The drawings, without the baronial tower (an effective afterthought) are still in the house. Inside, all rooms open off a double height Gothic hall. It was bought by the late Major Robert Aldridge and his wife in 1932. Now run by Mrs Aldridge.

Gravad Lax

Clean and fillet about an 8lb (3.6 kilo) salmon; if possible do not wash it.

6 level tablespoons sugar
6 level tablespoons salt
3 tablespoons white pepper
plenty of dill

Sprinkle the salt mixture on a sheet of greaseproof paper. Add a layer of dill stalks. Press more salt mixture onto the cut sides of both fillets, place one fillet on the greaseproof paper, skin side down. Cover this with plenty of dill. Place the next fillet, cut side down, on top; sprinkle on the rest of the salt. Cover with dill and wrap the fish up in the greaseproof paper. Then wrap it all in a parcel of tin foil with a light weight on top. Put in a very cool place but not the fridge. Turn the fish once and leave for 48 hours.

It is now ready to eat. Carefully scrape off all the salt mixture and dill. Wipe it but do not wash it. Cut in thin slices like smoked salmon. Serve with dill sauce.

Jugged Hare

'We have a constant supply of French shooters who give me hares to cook and this is their favourite dish,'said Mrs Aldridge. 'I make hare soup with the same flavourings which is also very popular.'

1 hare cut off the bone (but left in large pieces). Keep the blood and liver
2 oz (55 g)/2 rashers streaky bacon
butter for frying
thyme, bay-leaf, parsley, cloves, peppercorns
marmalade
red wine
lemon juice if needed
onions

Boil up the bones for stock. Roll the meat in seasoned flour and brown in a little butter along with the onions and bacon. Take out the meat, add enough flour to soak up the fat. Add the stock and all the herbs, bring to the boil and stir for a few minutes. Pour this and the meat into a heavy casserole and boil for 2 hours on a slow heat

until very tender. Add blood, mashed liver, red wine, marmalade and lemon juice if needed. I prefer wine and marmalade to port and redcurrant jelly. Keep tasting for the right flavour, adding whatever is needed until it is just right.

Treacle Tart

Bake blind a pastry case, preferably on a tin plate. In a small saucepan melt just enough golden syrup to cover the pastry case; add a few drops of almond essence and a dash of lemon juice. Fill the pastry case with fine white breadcrumbs and pour syrup mixture over the top. Make sure there are enough crumbs to exactly soak up the syrup so you can cut it without it being runny. Before eating sprinkle on a little ground almonds and a thin layer of crumbled cornflakes.

Coopershill House

COOPERSHILL HOUSE COMBINES ALL THE ELEGANCE of the Georgian era with the amenities of today. In the cooler evenings blazing fires and sparkling candelabra give a cheerful air and ponderous family portraits look down on the guests enjoying their nightcaps before retiring to their regal bedrooms. The extensive park, garden and working-farm make the perfect setting. Winner of the 1987 Good Hotel Guide Cesar Award for 'Outstanding Irish Hospitality'.

Coopershill House, Coopershill, Riverstown, Co. Sligo.
Tel: 071-65108. Fax: 071-65466.
Telex: 40301 (attn. Coopershill).

Reservations: In USA call Robert Reid associates on 800-223-6510 (Toll Free). From USA and elsewhere call Coopershill direct by phone or Fax.
Proprietors: Brian and Lindy O'Hara.
Open 16 March to 1 November.
Out of season house parties by arrangement.

How to find
Signed from Drumfin Crossroads, 11 miles south west of Sligo on route N4 to Dublin.

Restaurant
Dinner IR£16 at 8 pm. No service charge.

Accommodation
Bed and breakfast IR£32.
No. of bedrooms: 6.
All major credit cards accepted.

Palladian house, designed by Francis Bindon, and built 1755-1774. It is Co. Sligo's most spectacular, surviving 18th century private house. Original four poster beds in all the bedrooms except one. Chests full of muslin dresses and brocades, all undisturbed through centuries of unbroken family ownership, still exist.

Tomato Orange Soup

1 medium onion, chopped
1 tablespoon oil
1 rasher bacon, diced
1 14 oz (400 g) tin tomatoes
2 tablespoons cornflour
½ teaspoon paprika
½ teaspoon dried oregano
½ teaspoon sugar
1 tablespoon tomato purée
salt and pepper
2 pints (1.2 litres)/5 cups chicken stock
juice of one orange
cream to garnish

Soften the onion in the oil. Add the rasher, then the tomatoes and cook together for about 5 minutes.

Place cornflour, paprika, oregano, sugar, and tomato purée in a blender and add hot tomato mixture. Blend until smooth. Return to saucepan, add the chicken stock, and simmer for 10 minutes stirring from time to time. Stir in the orange juice and adjust seasoning; serve with a little cream to give a marbled effect for garnish.

Pork Chops Macon

1 pork loin chop per person
salt and pepper
French mustard
2 tablespoons oil
6 fl oz/(170 ml)/⅔ cup white wine
2 tablespoons soured cream
3 tablespoon fresh breadcrumbs
1 tablespoon chopped parsley

Season chops on both sides with salt and pepper. Spread one side of chops with mustard and set aside in a cool place for at least one hour.

Brown chops on both sides in the oil (reserving the pan and oil for browning the breadcrumbs later) and transfer to an ovenproof dish or casserole. Add the white wine, cover tightly and cook in a moderate oven 350°F/180°C/Regulo 4 for 45 minutes to 1 hour. During the last fifteen minutes baste chops with the soured cream and return, uncovered, to the oven. Toss breadcrumbs in oil left from browning the chops and sprinkle with the parsley on top of the chops and serve.

Caramel Mousse

4 oz (110 g)/½ cup granulated sugar
3 eggs plus 2 egg yolks
4 oz (110 g)/½ cup castor sugar
4 teaspoons powdered gelatine
½ pint (300 ml)/1¼ cups double cream, whipped
4 fl oz (120 ml)/½ cup water

Put the granulated sugar in a heavy pan with 4 tablespoons cold
water. Heat gently until the sugar dissolves, then bring to the boil
and cook to a rich chestnut-coloured caramel. Remove from heat
and carefully add the warm water (stand well back and cover your
hand with an oven glove in case the caramel splutters). Heat gently
until the caramel dissolves, then leave to cool.
Sprinkle the gelatine over the water in a small heatproof bowl and
leave for 5 minutes. Whisk the egg yolks and castor sugar together
until the mixture is very thick and light, and the whisk leaves a rib-
bon-like trail when lifted. Gently melt the gelatine by standing the
bowl in a pan of hot water. Stir the gelatine into the egg mixture,
fold in the cooled caramel and the whipped cream. When thoroughly blended, pour into the serving dish and leave to set in a cool
place. Serve with a compôte of sliced oranges or fresh fruit salad.

Reveries Restaurant

DECORATED IN STUNNING SHADES OF BLUE, Reveries is extended out in a series of tiers descending the hillside. The extension was built mainly in glass to capture the night sky through the roof and the panorama of the Atlantic Ocean with its coastal islands and Yeats's Knocknarea through the glass walls. Outside, the Atlantic can do its worst – you are cocooned in star-studded comfort, enjoying food and wine which are amongst the best in the west.

Reveries, Rosses Point, Sligo.
Tel: 071-77371

Reservations: Helpful but not necessary to 071-77371.
Proprietors: Damien Brennan and Paula Gilvarry.
Open Tuesday to Saturday. Dinner only.
Closed 2 weeks Nov. and four days Christmas.

How to find
Centre of Rosses Point village (6 miles north of Sligo city).

Restaurant
Dinner only from 7.30 pm.
Menu table d'hôte from IR£14.75.
10% service charge.
Credit cards: Access, Mastercard, Visa.

Reveries grew from a little old mews house in Rosses Point with
not much going for it except the sensational views. From this the
present owners built a restaurant which is an inspired
blend of old and new.

Curried Celery and Apple Soup

3 oz (85 g)/⅓ cup butter
5 oz (140 g) onion, peeled and chopped
1½ lb (675 g) celery, chopped
1½ lb (675 g) eating apples, washed and cored
1½ tablespoons mild curry powder
3 medium potatoes, peeled and chopped
3 pints (1.2 litres)/5 cups chicken stock
salt and pepper

Melt the butter in a large saucepan. Add the onion and sweat for 5-6 minutes. Add the celery and apple and cook for a few more minutes and then add the curry powder and cook for 10 minutes. Add the potatoes and stock and cook until the vegetables are soft. Purée and sieve. Season to taste. Reheat and serve with buttery croûtons and cubes of sweet apple.

Medallions of Pork with Creamy Basil Sauce

3 pork fillets
4 tomatoes
1 large onion, chopped
1 large clove garlic, crushed
3 oz (85 g)/⅓ cup butter
3 teaspoons fresh basil, chopped
6 oz (170 g) breadcrumbs

Preheat the oven to 350°F/180°C/Regulo 4.
Trim the pork fillets and cut into thick medallions, (about six per person). De-seed the tomatoes and cut into small dice. Sweat the onions and garlic in butter, add the tomatoes, basil and bread-crumbs. Mix well. Place a teaspoon of this topping on each piece of pork and place on a roasting tray. Bake for 20-30 minutes.
To serve: pour the sauce onto the plate, then put the pork in a circle on the plate and garnish with a basil leaf.

Sauce

    8 fl oz (250 ml)/1 cup chicken stock

    6 tablespoons white wine

    8 fl oz (250 ml)/1 cup cream

    4 teaspoons pesto

    salt and pepper

Simmer to reduce the stock and wine by half, add the cream and reduce by half again. Stir in pesto and season.

Pesto

    2 tablespoons toasted pine nuts

    2 oz (55 g) fresh basil leaves

    2 cloves garlic, peeled

    4 fl oz (120 ml)/½ cup good olive oil

Process to a paste in a food processor and use as above. Any leftover will keep in a jar in the fridge for several months.

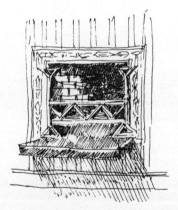

Blackcurrant Jelly with Orange Flower Sauce

If fresh blackcurrants are used, cook with the sugar and proceed as for tinned.

  2 tins blackcurrants (unsweetened)
  4 oz (110 g)/½ cup castor sugar
  3 fl oz (85 ml)/⅓ cup cassis or ½ cup Ribena and ½ cup white wine
  ½ oz (15 g) gelatine
  2 tablespoons water

Dissolve the gelatine in the 2 tablespoons water.
Strain the juice from the blackcurrants into a measuring jug, add sugar and dissolve. Add the cassis and enough water to measure up to 1¼ pints/750 ml. Heat gently in a saucepan and mix in the soaked gelatine. Strain into a wetted mould or six small moulds. Leave overnight in the fridge. To unmould, dip the mould into hot water for a few seconds, invert onto a serving dish, give a few firm shakes and lift off the mould.

Orange Flower Sauce

  2 egg yolks
  2 oz (55 g)/¼ cup castor sugar
  8 fl oz (250 ml)/1 cup cream
  1 tablespoon orange flower water

Whisk the egg yolks and sugar together until creamy. In a heavy-bottomed saucepan, heat the cream until just simmering, then whisk into the egg yolks. Return to the saucepan and cook over a low heat until the mixture coats the back of a wooden spoon. Remove from the heat and add the flower water. Cool, stirring occasionally.

Ernan Park

ST ERNAN'S HOUSE (NOW ERNAN PARK), on the eight-and-a-half acre St Ernan's Island near Donegal town, is close to some of the most beautiful scenery in this scenic county. Its creator sited his house on the low point of the island to protect it from the wild Atlantic winter gales. He built protective walls so that he could cultivate trees, and laid out attractive walks around his little domain.

The restored interior of this manor house is strikingly beautiful with antiquity, colour and pattern inspiringly blended. As befits such a house, service is personal and charming.

The views along the Atlantic coast are of miniature white farm houses and tiny sheep dotting the distant hills like a stage setting. It is an image of Ireland that people dream about. The gracious dining room glows with warmth. The cuisine is well-nigh perfect. To stay at Ernan Park is to live a little.

St. Ernan's House Hotel, St. Ernan's Island, Donegal, Co. Donegal. Tel: 0073-21065. Fax: 073-22098.

Reservations: In USA call Robert Reid Associates or direct.
Proprietors: Brian and Carmel O'Dowd.
Open from Easter to end of October.
Children under 6 not catered for.

How to find
2 miles south of Donegal town.

Restaurant
Dinner (5 course) IR£17.50, served from 6.30-8.30 pm.
No service charge.

Accommodation
Bed and breakfast with bath IR£28-IR£39.50.
No. of bedrooms: 11.
Visa and Access accepted.

The house, situated on the tidal island of St Ernan's, was built in
1826 by John Hamilton, a nephew of the Duke of Wellington.
He was noted for his kindness to the tenants on his large estate
and, untypical of his kind, he ran up huge debts to feed them
during the Famine. After the Famine, his grateful tenants built a
causeway to the island as a token of their appreciation. This
causewaynow gives motor access to the house.
St Ernan's became a hotel in 1983.

Stuffed Aubergine

3 aubergines (eggplant)
salt

Stuffing
3 oz (85 g)/⅓ cup butter
3 oz (85 g) onion, diced
6 oz (170 g) mushrooms, diced
1½ oz (45 g) sage, parsley, thyme and rosemary mixed
6 oz (170 g) white breadcrumbs
6 oz (170 g) white cheddar cheese, grated

Preheat the oven to 350°F/180°C/Regulo 4.
Cut the aubergines in half lengthwise, rub with salt and leave to
drain on a wire rack for 30 minutes. Rinse in cold water and bake
for 8-10 minutes. Cool.

Stuffing
Melt the butter and cook the onions and mushrooms gently, add
the herbs and simmer for 5 minutes. Mix in the breadcrumbs. Cool.
Scoop out the centre of the aubergines, and retain the skins. Cut the
aubergine flesh into fine dice, mix with the rest of the stuffing and
season. Refill the aubergine skins. Top with cheese and bake in the
oven until brown.

Baked John Dory with Fennel Sauce

12 medium John Dory fillets skinned
3 oz butter softened
3 teaspoons Pernod

Preheat the oven to 350°F/180°C/Regulo 4.
Place the fillets on a greased baking sheet. Mix butter and Pernod
together and place a little on top of each fillet. Bake for 5-10
minutes.

Fennel Sauce

- 10 oz (285 g)/1¼ cups butter
- 10 oz (285 g) onion
- 2 oz (55 g) fennel
- 1 pint (600 ml)/2½ cups cream
- salt and black pepper

Melt the butter, add the onion and fennel and cook gently. Season. Strain off any excess liquid and add the cream. Reduce by half and adjust the seasoning. Serve with watercress, cucumber and lemon wedges.

Strawberry Cheesecake with Irish Whiskey

3 oz (85 g) / ⅓ cup unsalted butter
3 tablespoons honey
9 oz (250 g) oatmeal biscuits crushed

Topping

1 lb 5 oz (600 g) full fat cream cheese
3 tablespoons Irish whiskey
8 fl oz (250 ml) / 1 cup cream
6 tablespoons honey
1 lb (450 g) strawberries

Line an 8½ inch (22 cm) cheesecake or springform tin. Melt the butter and honey over a low heat. Stir in the biscuit crumbs. Press the mixture into the tin and chill for 1 hour.

Topping

Mix cream cheese and whiskey until smooth. Whisk in the cream and stir in the honey. Crush the strawberries, reserving about six for decoration, and fold into the cheese mixture. Spoon the topping onto the base, chill for 2-3 hours until firm, then decorate with remaining strawberries.

Rathmullan House

THE MOST NORTHERLY OF THE COUNTRY HOUSES – (you can't get much further north than Lough Swilly). County Donegal is one of Ireland's most beautiful counties. The garden at Rathmullan is a joy, lovingly cared for by generations of Irish men and women. With such a spectacular view from the dining room, it is hard to concentrate on your plate. The food is traditional and super-abundant, with salmon, trout, Donegal lamb and beef much in evidence – beautiful food eaten in beautiful surroundings. The hotel is one of the largest of the Country House Hotels and is a relaxed and comfortable place for a long or short stay.

Rathmullan House, Rathmullan, Letterkenny, Co. Donegal.
Tel: 074-58188. Fax: 074-58200.

Reservations: Robert Reid Associates 800-223-6510 (Toll Free).
Proprietors: Bob and Robin Wheeler.
Open 17 March to Christmas (excl.)

How to find
Take Ramelton road (T72) from Letterkenny. Turn right after bridge in Ramelton (L77) to Rathmullan.

Restaurant
Sunday buffet lunch from IR£10, 1-2 pm.
Dinner 7.30-8.30 pm from IR£14.50. 10% service charge.

Accommodation
Bed and breakfast from IR£30.
No. of bedrooms: 18.
All major credit cards accepted.

*Rathmullan House was the seaside residence of the Batt family.
A Regency villa of 1837 vintage, doubled in size in 1880 so that
there are two front doors. An equally amiable eccentric interior
culminates in a Hindu Gothic dining-room recalling the family
sojourn in India. The spacious gardens slope down through rare
trees to a sandy beach with a view of the mountains across the
lough. Interior decoration of the house is by the present
owners, Robin and Bob Wheeler.*

141

Mushroom Croustades

For 24 croustades
These are small breadcases with a delicious filling of mushrooms. They need to be prepared in advance and made ready to put in the oven ten minutes before being served. Use a food processor to chop the shallots/onions and mushrooms. They will keep quite happily in a warm oven for 20-30 minutes.

Breadcases
For 24 bun tins
   12 slices white bread
   1 oz (30 g)/2 tablespoons soft butter
Coat the inside of a bun sheet with butter. Using a 2½ inch (6.5 cm) cutter make two rounds from each slice of bread. Press firmly and neatly into each bun tin. Bake in a preheated oven, 400°F/200°C/Regulo 6 for 10 minutes. Cool on a wire rack. Any not used will keep in an air-tight tin.

The Filling

   2 oz (55 g)/¼ cup butter
   3 tablespoons shallots/spring onions, finely chopped
   ½ lb (225 g)/2½ cups mushrooms, finely chopped
   2 level tablespoons flour
   ½ pint (300 ml)/1¼ cups cream
   ½ teaspoon salt
   pinch cayenne
   1 tablespoon chopped parsley
   1 ½ tablespoons chopped chives
   ½ teaspoon lemon juice
   a little grated parmesan cheese
   butter
Melt butter in frying pan, cook shallots/spring onions for about 5 minutes without browning. Add mushrooms and stir well. Allow to cook until all the moisture has evaporated. Remove pan from heat. Mix the flour in well and add the cream. Stir continuously and bring to the boil for a minute or two. Off the heat, add the seasonings, herbs and lemon juice. Turn into a bowl and refrigerate for at least 4 hours.

142

To serve: Fill each case. Sprinkle with a little parmesan cheese. Dot
with the extra butter. Place on baking sheet and heat in preset oven
350°F/180°C/Regulo 4 for 10 minutes.
The filling will keep for 2-3 days well-covered in the fridge.

Gooseberry Sorbet

17½ fl oz (545 mls)/ 2 cups water
1 lb 2 oz (500 g)/2¼ cups sugar
1 lb 2 oz (500 g) gooseberries
1 egg white

Bring the sugar and water to the boil gently, making sure the sugar
is dissolved. Boil for 1 minute. Stew gooseberries in a little water
until soft. Liquidise and rub through a fine sieve. Mix with syrup.
Add white of egg and churn in an ice cream maker. Alternatively
place mixture without white of egg in deep freeze and leave until
slushy. Add stiffly beaten white of egg and return to freezer.

Poached Salmon

Nowadays salmon is available all year round with the marketing of
farm-bred fish. Spring salmon is still the finest for flavour. Serve it
just warm or make sure it has had time to soften after refrigeration.
To cook make up a salmon bath of water with salt, peppercorns,
parsley stalks, thinly sliced onion and lemon, sliced carrot and
celery, bay leaves, thyme and fennel, simmer for 5 minutes. The
fish is placed in the bath and poached with hardly any movement
of the liquid. A 10 lb (4.5 kilo) fish takes approx 1¼ hours.
Later in the season add olive oil to the water when the salmon
tends to get drier. The salmon can be served with a herb hollan-
daise, mayonnaise, or brown butter. Excellent served with new potatoes and a salad.

Little Chocolate Pots

Use the small *pot au chocolat* for this pudding, although any small dishes will do. They do need to be small, as this is a very rich mousse.

   12 oz (340 g) dark chocolate
   6 tablespoons water
   1 oz (30 g)/2 tablespoons butter
   2 dessertspoons rum
   6 eggs (separated)

Melt the chocolate and water over low heat. Add butter and rum off the heat. Separate 6 eggs and add each yolk separately, stirring in well. Whisk the egg whites to firm snow and stir in briskly. Fill containers; you can use a jug for this. Keep for a day before using. They will keep for at least a week in the fridge. The chocolate needs to be the best dark chocolate you can get.

Blackheath House

BLACKHEATH HOUSE REMAINED IN CHURCH HANDS for 100 years before being bought as a private estate by the Rothwell family. Its heyday appears to have been during the long encumbancies of the Rev. Alexander followed by his son-in-law Dean Andrew Smyly during the years 1832-1880. Rev. Alexander became Primate of All Ireland, and his wife Cecil (1818-1895), a noted poet, wrote many famous hymns including – 'There is a Green Hill Far Away', 'All Things Bright and Beautiful', and 'Once in Royal David's City'.

The hotel-restaurant (MacDuffs) is situated within the six counties of Northern Ireland adjacent to the scenic coastline of Londonderry and the Giant's Causeway. The bedrooms are stylish and endowed with colour television and en suite bathrooms – (amenities I am sure the 18th century rectors would have frowned upon). The food and service however reflect the standards of past centuries with local game, seafood and fresh garden and farm produce cooked with great care, something which is rare in these hurried times.

Blackheath House, 112 Killeague Road, Blackhill, Coleraine,
Co. Londonderry BT51 4HH.
Tel: 0265-868433.

From Republic of Ireland telephone: (08) 0265-868433.
Reservations: Robert Reid Associates.

Proprietors: Joseph and Margaret Erwin.
Open all year except Christmas.
Children under 12 not catered for.

How to find
Just off A29 4 miles north of Garvagh and 7 miles south of Coleraine.

Restaurant
Dinner 7.00-9.30 pm from IR£15.

Accommodation
Bed and breakfast only Sunday and Monday.
Bed and breakfast from IR£25 single; IR£45 double.
No. of bedrooms: 6.
N.I.T.B. Grade A.

Blackheath House was built as the Glebe House of the parish of
St Guaire in 1795 by the Earl Bishop of Bristol, for one of his
nephews. It is attributed to Cork architect Michael Shanahan. The
facade of two stories conceals a structure of four floors – a compact
and commodious plan characteristic of Irish rectories. Acquired by
Joseph and Margaret Erwin and restored by them in 1978 first as
a private house and later converted into a country
house hotel and restaurant.

Prawn Puffs with Side Salad and Ohio Sauce

   1 lb (450 g) cooked prawns
   ¾ lb (340 g) puff pastry
   seasoning

Roll out the pastry finely. Using a tea plate cut six round shapes. Cover half the pastry with prawns and seasoning, fold over top to make a semi-circle and press edges together with a little water. Turn until the fluted edge is on top like a pasty; coat with beaten egg. Cook in a hot oven for ten minutes or until pastry is cooked. Serve at once with a side salad garnish and cold savoury sauces. For example, tartare sauce, Marie Rose, or Ohio Sauce (as below).

Ohio Sauce

   1 large onion
   1 lb (450 g) jar preserved beetroot
   2 tablespoons mayonnaise
   2 oz (55 g) / ¼ cup Philadelphia cheese
   cream

Cut and boil onion in the vinegar from beetroot jar, then add the beetroot, purée in a food processor with the Philadelphia. Add the mayonnaise and a little cream to taste. Will keep well in a covered container if refrigerated.

Rack of Lamb with Mulled Wine Sauce

2 racks of lamb, enough to give three cutlets per person

Have the butcher cut through the bone. Cut six joints of three cutlets each. Remove fat from bone end of joint and score the remainder in a criss-cross pattern. Cook on a tray in a hot oven for 10 minutes to crisp the fat and then in a moderate oven until the meat is cooked to your preference. Carve each joint and serve on individual plates decorated with fresh herbs, mulled wine sauce and seasonal fruits e.g. redcurrants, plums, or blackberries.

Mulled Wine Sauce

4 tablespoons redcurrant jelly

2 tablespoons port

2 glasses red wine

½ teaspoon cinnamon

½ teaspoon ginger

½ teaspoon nutmeg

juice of 1 lemon

juice of 1 orange

Combine all ingredients together in a saucepan and let simmer until the jelly has melted. Continue to cook until the mixture is reduced by half and has a good flavour. If further thickening is required use a little arrowroot and water.

Athol Brose – a Scottish dessert of which there are many variations

1 pint (600 ml)/2½ cups stiffly whipped cream
3 tablespoons soft runny honey
2 tablespoons muesli
4 tablespoons whisky – or to taste

Gently fold in muesli with the cream, add the honey and lastly the whisky. Stir carefully. Transfer to individual glasses. Decorate with toasted oatmeal. Chill and serve with flakemeal biscuits.

Flakemeal Biscuits

4 oz (110 g)/½ cup margarine
2 oz (55 g)/¼ cup sugar
2 oz (55 g)/½ cup flour
½ teaspoon salt
5 oz (140 g)/1⅓ cups flakemeal (porridge oats)
pinch of bicarbonate soda

Mix all ingredients in a food processor. Roll out and cut biscuits into required shapes. Bake at 350-375 ℉/180-190℃/Regulo 4-5 for approximately 20 minutes. Sprinkle with sugar.

Architectural Notes

The country houses and restaurants illustrated here represent a narrow cross-section of Irish domestic architecture, but they suggest a solution to the conservation of the remainder.

Few historic houses can survive on their takings at the door. They may provide the owners with their supper but cannot mend the roof. Open in this way they are so often empty shells; but when they open their doors to guests, offering four-poster beds, as well as fish and game served by candlelight, they spring to life again, with their visitors no longer voyeurs but participators. They are not only preserved, but enjoyed.

Why then has the Irish Country House and Restaurant Association received so little recognition in Ireland, so much at variance with its success abroad? These country houses pre-date 'official tourism' with their sources in either Edwardian shooting lodges of the West, or in the lush farmlands and walled gardens of Munster. Since they were never standardised in the 1960s they require to be treated with special sensitivity by whoever is in charge of the local by-laws. They are remarkable in the resourcefulness and independent-mindedness of each proprietor. Twenty-five of the owners are their own architects, nearly all tend their own gardens and organise their own interior decoration while at least three houses contain large collections of paintings by close relatives. Among the paintings, there is occasionally a tribute from a guest, a record of an afternoon's enchantment.

The drawings in this book are in that tradition. They are portraits of houses. What I have stressed is not so much the architecture as their inner ambience and outward setting. So many of these houses are sited over water that magically reflects them. Having captured it only by balancing precariously over a very strong and cold November current, can one appreciate the original skill of the builder in linking house to landscape.

Index

Almond.
  Almond Roll 70
  Almond and Walnut Cake 110
  Walnut and Almond Gâteau 39
Apple.
  Apple Pie du 'Parc' 79
  Cinnamon Apple Flan 120
  Individually Cooked Apple Tarts 24
Apricot.
  Apricot Mousse 20
Artichokes.
  Artichauts Farci 47
Athol Brose. 149
Aubergine.
  Stuffed Aubergine 137
Avocado.
  Avocado in Puff Pastry with a Fresh Tomato Sauce 77
  Avocado Sauce 91
  Avocado Sorbet 95
Biscuits.
  Flakemeal Biscuits 149
Blackcurrant.
  Blackcurrant Jelly with Orange Flower Sauce 134
  Irish Blackcurrant Cream 74
Broccoli.
  Broccoli Soup with Garlic Croûtons 119
Chicken.
  Brochette of Fruit and Chicken with Avocado Sauce 90
  Chicken or Game Consommé 23
  Chicken with Orange and Mustard Sauce 104
  Chicken Valencia with Pine Nuts 47-8
  Parslied Chicken Guerard 114-15
Chocolate.
  Chocolate Praline Pudding 100
  Chocolate Profiteroles with Banana Cream 15-16
  Joe's Favourite Chocolate Cake 65-6
  Little Chocolate Pots 144
Crab.
  Artichauts Farci 47
  Crab Claws Malibu 27-8
  Devilled Crab Cakes with Tarragon Sauce ,86

Crème Brûlée. 116
Duck.
    Piccatas of Duck Liver Foie Gras 73
    Ribbons of Wild Duckbreast with Two Sauces 77-8
Fish. *See also Salmon; Trout*
    Baked John Dory with Fennel Sauce 137-8
    Fillets of Black Sole Rosas 59
    Fish Cream 60
    Grilled Oysters 19
    Poached Fillet of Brill with a Fresh Basil Sauce 64
    Sea Bass Baked in Orange Juice and White Wine 51
    Seafood Pâté 103
Fruits.
    Autumn Pudding 34
    Framboise 48
Game.
    Chicken or Game Consommé 23
    Game terrine with Gooseberry Chutney 59
Gâteaux.
    Walnut and Almond Gâteau 39
Goose.
    Stuffed Goose 19
Gooseberries.
    Gooseberry Chutney 59
    Gooseberry Sorbet 143
Hare.
    Jugged Hare 123-4
Icecream.
    Vanilla Icecream with Fresh Fruit in Season 60
Lamb.
    Boiled Leg of Lamb with Caper Sauce 73
    Lamb in a Basil Sauce 'aux petits légumes' 23
    Lambs' Brains Schoolhouse Style 37
    Lamb Roast with Irish Garden Herbs 55
    Rack of Lamb with Mulled Wine Sauce 148
Lemons.
    Lemon Sauce 99
    Tarte au Citron 43-4
Lettuce.
    Lettuce and Mint Soup 54
    Mussels in a Lettuce Sauce 94
    Salade de Pigeon 42
Mangoes.
    Mango and Raspberry Coulis 24

Meringues.
'Swan Lake' Meringues 28-9
Mousse.
Apricot Mousse 20
Caramel Mousse 129
Scallop Mousse with Beurre Blanc Sauce 82
Smoked Salmon Mousse 69
Yoghurt Mousse with Pineapple, Strawberries or Kiwi Fruit and a Caramel Sauce 104-105
Mushrooms.
Mushroom Croustades 142-3
Mussels.
Mussels in a Lettuce Sauce 94
Oranges.
Oranges in Grand Marnier 91
Oysters.
Grilled Oysters 19
Oysters with Quail Eggs and Sour Cream Dressing 32
Pâtés.
Seafood Pâté 103
Pears.
Pear Cake 83
Pheasant.
Roast Pheasant and Game 'Jus' 94
Pigeon.
Pigeon Breast with Lime and Peppery Pineapple 37-8
Pigeon Pie 14
Salade de Pigeon 42
Pork.
Medallions of Pork with Creamy Basil Sauce 132-3
Pork Chops Macon 127-8
Pork Fillets Stuffed with Prunes 32-3
Prawns.
Flambéed Union Hall Prawns with Mushrooms 64
Fresh Prawns En-croûte with Provençale Sauce 113
Prawn Puffs with Side Salad and Ohio Sauce 147
Raspberries.
Mango and Raspberry Coulis 24
Framboise 48
Salmon.
Aherne's Hot Potato and Smoked Salmon Starter 51
Darne de Saumon aux Pointes D'Asperges 42
Gravad Lax 123
Poached Salmon 143

Smoked Salmon Mousse 69
Terrine of Smoked Salmon 98
Sauces.
    Avocado 91
    Beurre Blanc 82
    Caramel 105
    Creamy Basil Sauce 133
    Fennel 138
    Fresh Basil 23,64
    Juniper Berry 78
    Lemon 99
    Mulled Wine 148
    Ohio 147
    Orange Flower Sauce 134
    Pinekernel 78
    Provençale 113
    Tarragon 86
    Tomato 77
    White Wine 60
    Yoghurt and Herb 119
Sausages.
    Home Smoked Sausages 90
Scallops.
    Scallop Mousse with Beurre Blanc Sauce 82
Soufflé.
    Fresh Strawberry 87
    Irish Mist 55-6
Soups.
    Broccoli Soup with Garlic Croûtons 119
    Carrot and Onion Soup 14
    Chicken or Game Consommé 23
    Curried Celery and Apple Soup 132
    Lettuce and Mint Soup 54
    Mulligatawny Soup 108
    Potato and Ham Soup 27
    Tomato Orange Soup 127
Strawberries.
    Fresh Strawberry Soufflé 87
    Strawberry Cheesecake with Irish Whiskey 139
Tarts.
    Tarte au Citron 43-4
    Treacle Tart 124
Terrines.
    Game Terrine with Gooseberry Chutney 59
    Terrine of Smoked Salmon 98

Trout.
    Brown Trout with Mushroom Sauce 82-3
    Hot Smoked Trout with Yoghurt and Herb Sauce 119
Turkey.
    Stuffed Turkey Breton Style 110
Veal.
    Baked Stuffed Leg of Veal with Lemon Sauce 98-9
    Escalopes of Veal stuffed with Sweetbreads in a Mushroom
        Cream Sauce 69-70
    Veal Steaks with Lemon 87

IRELAND
Location Map

Other books from The O'Brien Press

Pictorial Ireland
Yearbook and Appointments Diary
Superb full colour photographs of Ireland's wonderful
landscapes, towns, people. Each year a new diary, available
every summer in advance. *Wiro bound £6.95.*

Irish Life and Traditions
Ed. Sharon Gmelch
Visions of contemporary Ireland from some of its most
well-known commentators — Maeve Binchy, Nell McCaf-
ferty, Seán Mac Réamoinn, Seán MacBride. Deals with nature, cities, prehistory, growing up in Ireland (from the
1890s in Clare to the 1960s in Derry), sports, fairs, festivals,
words spoken and sung. 256 pages, 200 photos.
£6.95 paperback.

Old Days Old Ways
Olive Sharkey
Entertaining and informative illustrated folk history, re-
counting the old way of life in the home and on the land.
Full of charm. *£5.95 paperback.*

Kerry
Des Lavelle and Richard Haughton
The landscape, legends, history and people of a beautiful
county. Stunning full colour photographs. *£5.95 paperback.*

Sligo
Land of Yeats' Desire
John Cowell
An evocative account of the history, literature, folklore and
landscapes, with eight guided tours of the city and county,
from one who spent his childhood days in the Yeats
country in the early years of this century. Illustrated. *£14.95
hardback.*

A Valley of Kings
THE BOYNE
Henry Boylan
An inspired guide to the myths, magic and literature of this
beautiful valley with its mysterious 5000-year-old monu-
ments at Newgrange. Illustrated. *£7.95 paperback.*

Traditional Irish Recipes
George L. Thomson
Handwritten in beautiful calligraphy, a collection of fa-
vourite recipes from the Irish tradition. *£3.95 paperback.*

Consumer Choice Guide to Restaurants in Ireland
With the Consumer Association of Ireland
About 300 restaurants assessed by consumers from all over
the country. An essential guide for the traveller.
£4.95 paperback.

THE BLASKET ISLANDS — Next Parish America
Joan and Ray Stagles
The history, characters, social organisation, nature - all
aspects of this most fascinating and historical of islands.
Illustrated. *£7.95 paperback.*

SKELLIG — Island outpost of Europe
Des Lavelle
Probably Europe's strangest monument from the Early
Christian era, this island, several miles out to sea, was the
home of an early monastic settlement. Illustrated.
£7.95 paperback.

DUBLIN — One Thousand Years
Stephen Conlin
A short history of Dublin with unique full colour recon-
struction drawings based on the latest research.
Hardback £9.95, paperback £5.95.